# WHY DID I DO THAT?

*Freeing Your*
*God-given*
*Emotions*

James A. May
&
Dianne May

Paulist Press
New York/Mahwah, NJ

Cover and book design by Lynn Else

Library of Congress Cataloging-in-Publication Data

May, James A., 1923–
    Why did I do that? : freeing your God-given emotions / James A. May & Dianne May.
        p.    cm.
    Includes bibliographical references.
    ISBN 978-0-8091-4483-9 (alk. paper)
    1. Emotions—Religious aspects—Christianity. 2. Change (Psychology)—Religious aspects—Christianity. I. May, Dianne. II. Title.
BV4597.3.M38 2007
248.8'6—dc22

                                                                    2007006263

Published by Paulist Press
997 Macarthur Boulevard
Mahwah, New Jersey 07430

www.paulistpress.com

Printed and bound in the
United States of America

# Contents

## Part III Troubleshooting

# Introduction

St. Paul wanted to change. He told the Romans in his letter, "I do not understand my own actions. For I do not do what I want, but I do the very thing I hate" (Romans 7:15). Like us, St. Paul must have asked himself, "Why did I *do* that?" Like St. Paul, we rely on God's grace. But God's grace can guide us to many insights into the human condition developed by modern psychotherapy.

Jim practiced psychotherapy for over sixty years. He worked with CEOs and welfare mothers, football players and poets. What they all had in common was a desire to change their lives in some way. Jim helped them do that. He helped people to free themselves from the emotions and habits that distressed them. He showed them ways of changing that really work. Jim retired a few years ago. Since then, many people have asked him what they can do to change their lives. We wrote this book to tell them.

There are two ways to read this book. Both ways work. Chapters 1 through 10 explain the ideas that make it easier for people to change. If you are curious about how human nature works, you will probably enjoy reading this section. Because these first ten chapters form the foundation for the rest of the book, it is helpful to start at the beginning and read straight through. This will give you an understanding of the techniques that we present in later chapters and allow you to use those techniques creatively.

Some people, however, are more practical-minded. You may want to turn directly to Chapter 11 and begin there with suggestions about what to do. If you find something that you don't quite understand, you can turn back to the earlier chapters. Chapters 11 through 17 give practical techniques for changing. In Chapters 18 through 22, we discuss specific problems that many people struggle with. You may want to turn to one of these chapters first.

As you read our book, you will notice that sometimes we use the pronoun *he* and sometimes *she*. We did this not to confuse the reader, but as a way to be sensitive to the issue of gender inclusiveness.

Some of the ideas in this book may be unfamiliar. The concepts of the pleasure emotions, the pragmatic emotions, the intellect, and the will are as old as Aristotle and were familiar to the earliest Christians. These concepts played a central role in the Christian understanding of human nature for many centuries. Two Dutch Christian psychiatrists, Dr. Anna A. Terruwe and Dr. Conrad W. Baars, have given a modern explanation of these ideas, and we owe much to their work.

We also wrote this book for another reason. Over the years, we have noticed a feeling of deep distrust between the world of psychotherapy and the world of religion. Many people of different faiths perceive psychotherapy as hostile to religion. Many therapists perceive religion as the cause of people's unhappiness. We wanted to try to heal this rift. We know that faith and therapy work together to help people to grow and to love. We wrote this book for people of all faiths. We even hope to speak to professed atheists, letting them see that the god they do not believe in really does not exist, but that another God, a God of love and healing, does.

# PART I

# How It Works

# 1
# Why Did I Do That?

You weren't going to do that again. You made up your mind that this time it was going to be different. Then you found yourself eating a pint of ice cream, lighting up a cigarette, volunteering for another committee that you didn't have time for, or screaming at the kids. And you asked yourself, why did I *do* that?

Sometimes it seems as if there are two of you. The one with the good intentions and the determination to do it differently next time. And the other part of you that just doesn't want to change, the one that nags and whines until you give in and eat the ice cream, the one that starts yelling before you're even aware of it. You've tried will power. You've tried self-control. Maybe you've tried affirmations and behavior modification techniques. And that other part of you keeps on winning. You haven't been able to stop doing the things you hate doing.

How *can* we change? Sometimes we want to change our emotions. Sometimes we just want to change our actions. But *it is our emotions that lie at the root of our actions.* We may be uncomfortable with many of our emotions, even afraid of them. We're not sure what they really mean. All we know is that they trip us up. But what if we could change not just the emotions that trip us up? What if we could change the way all of our emotions work?

Our emotions were created to be *the power supporting and moving us* in what we want to do. Unfortunately our emotions don't do what they were created to do. They head out on their own, dragging us along behind them, and we find ourselves where we don't want to be, doing what we don't really want to

3

do. The more we try to control our emotions, the more they rebel. But emotions weren't created to be controlled. They were created to be guided. *We can learn how to guide our emotions so that the power they now have to drag us off in all directions can become the power to take us where we really want to go.*

How can we do this? First, we have to begin to think about our emotions in a new way. Some people see emotions as irrational forces within us and believe that emotions need to be controlled. Other people see emotions as the most authentic part of us, who we really are. Many of us hold both of these assumptions at the same time, believing that emotions such as joy or gratitude are real and good, but also wanting to get rid of feelings such as rage or fear. But there is a different way of seeing our emotions. *When we begin to see our emotions in this new way, we will find it easier to change.*

## Emotions Are a Way of Knowing

Our emotions begin in our senses. When we sense something, there is much more going on than just perceiving. *When we perceive something, our perception moves us to action, and that movement is called an emotion.* The action we take can be as simple as paying attention, or it can be as complex as writing a poem. The important point is that our emotions respond to our perceptions of the concrete, *material* world.

For example, we may be awakened in the middle of the night by an unfamiliar noise. Actually, we are not usually awakened by the sound, but rather by the jolt of fear that shoots through us. When we wake up, it is not because we are aware of the noise, but because we are aware of the fear that tells us that we need to identify a noise and decide how to deal with it. The perception of the unfamiliar noise and the emotion of fear are united. In fact, the feeling of fear is the body's way of knowing that danger may be near. *Our emotions are our body's way of knowing, and that knowing moves us to action.* We share this part of our being with the animals. It seems to us that animals have emotions because they do exhibit emotions similar to our own, although their emotions are limited to the material world while our emotions operate in the context of both material and spiritual realities. *In the material world of sensing and emotions, no emotion is good or bad, only correct or incorrect.* If what we sense largely corresponds with what is going on in the material world, the emotion that we feel will move us to a suitable action. If we are mistaken, our emotion will be inappropriate, and the action is likely to be inappropriate also.

We want to draw a very important distinction here between *two different kinds of emotions.* We do not mean that these two kinds of emotions are physiologically different, but rather that they function differently. This is a distinction that people are not used to making, but it is a critical one if we are going to understand what can go wrong with our emotions and what we can do about it. The *pleasure emotions,* the first kind, have to do with *what it is that we desire.* The second kind, the *pragmatic emotions,* have to do with figuring out *how to get what we desire.*

## Love, Desire, and Pleasure

The pleasure emotions—the emotions of love, desire, and pleasure—stand at the center of our being. *The pleasure emotions exist to move us toward what is good for us, toward what keeps us alive and well.* The first pleasure emotion is love. *Love* is the natural response to something we perceive to be good. It is the union in our mind with a good thing that we have perceived. It is reaching out and paying attention, bringing the good thing into our own awareness. We see food when we are hungry or a warm fire when we are cold and we simply say to ourselves, "That looks good."

What do we mean by good? That depends on your nature. If you are a sulfur-eating bacterium, then a hot vent spewing sulfuric fumes on the ocean floor is good for you. If you are a human being, it is not. Because we are human beings, certain things are good for us. Some plants (wheat or rice) are good for us to eat and some (poison ivy or poinsettia leaves) are not. A warm place to sleep out of the rain, the right kinds of food to eat, and a chance to reproduce are all good for us. Because they are good for us, we spontaneously say that we love a good fire, a hot meal, and someone to share it with. We love these things, just as animals love what is good for them. This is the material level of love.

In ordinary speech, we use the word *love* to cover a wide range of things—I love you, I love chocolate, I love dancing, I love that dress, I love God. Some people object to this. How, they ask, could we use the same term to describe both our feelings for chocolate and our feelings for God? Christianity distinguishes different kinds of love *(agape, philia, eros, storge)*, but it also recognizes that they are all love and that they are all related because they have to do with different kinds of *good.*

One kind of love is not more real than another. The sphere in which our emotions operate is the sphere of the senses, the material world, and *insofar as our emotions are responding to the material world, they are telling us real things about the material world and what is good in it*. In this sense, those who say that our emotions are neither good nor bad are correct. But human beings live in both the material world and the world of the spirit, so while our emotions can tell us about the material world, they cannot tell us about the spiritual world. Therefore, *while our emotions are not wrong in themselves, they are incomplete when we consider the entire context of human life.*

Even at the material level, love is not simple. Like all emotions, love involves both perception and action. The first step of love is the perception that something is good, good *for us,* and this is what is called *love in itself.* But love does not end there. Love is a force of unity, and we naturally want to be *really* united on the material level with the good thing. We do not just want to look at the chocolate, we want to eat it. We do not just want to see the fire in the distance, we want to put our hands right up next to it and feel its warmth. We do not just want to admire someone, we want to put our arms around her. This is called *desire,* and it is this part of love that moves us toward what we perceive as good. Without desire, nothing would ever happen.

What begins with love and continues in desire then ends in *pleasure.* Pleasure is what we experience when we are actually united with the good thing that we have perceived, when we are eating the chocolate, feeling the warmth of the fire, or making love. Pleasure means the resting of love in the possession of the material good that we have desired.

Love is a unifying force. It begins in the perception of the good, continues in the desire that moves us to the action that unites us with the good, and ends in the pleasure of enjoying the good. No creature can survive without this process. God created every human being to love, to desire, and to feel pleasure. *These pleasure emotions are the foundation of our entire emotional life.*

Once again, we must point out that in human beings these pleasure emotions exist within a larger context. In animals the pleasure emotions are complete in themselves. An animal enjoys what it has desired and rests until it desires again. Human beings feel love and desire in a much more complex context. The pleasure emotions are the foundation of our emotional life, but they are only a part of what we are.

## Negative Emotions

Of course not all of our emotions are enjoyable. We sometimes speak of negative emotions such as hate or fear, and many people assume that these emotions are bad or harmful in themselves. If we assume that these emotions are bad, we may try to eliminate them by denying them or stuffing them down, a process called repression. But these emotions are not bad in themselves. They have a positive and essential role to play in our lives. Just as the pleasure emotions are a response to what is good for us, what we may call negative emotions are a response to what we perceive as undesirable or bad for us. They are the opposite of the pleasure emotions, and *their purpose is to tell us in no uncertain terms that something is undesirable and to move us to appropriate action in response.*

*Hate* is the opposite of love. When we perceive something that is undesirable or bad for us, something that could harm us or that brings us suffering, the emotion that we feel in response to this is hate. Hate exists precisely to tell us that something is undesirable or bad for us. We say that we hate spoiled milk, smog, or someone who has slandered us.

It is common today to speak of hate crimes. The feelings underlying these acts are not the simple emotion of hate that we describe here. *When someone feels hate, it does not necessarily mean that what he hates is actually bad in itself.* For example, if a mother feels hate for her child, this does not mean that the child is bad. It may mean that the mother is feeling distress because of her own emotional and physical limitations in caring for her child, but since our emotional responses are responses only at the material level of reality, the *feeling* of hate does not understand that the child is not the problem. The feeling of hate is real, a response to demands on the mother that she finds overwhelming and distressing, and thus bad for her. Even if the mother knows that her child is not bad, she cannot experience the goodness of her child emotionally.

There are many words for hate, depending on the strength and cause of the hate. *Resentment,* for instance, is the hate we feel when we think we have been treated unfairly. Hate that comes from perceiving someone as an enemy is called *hostility.* We often mistake hate for anger. For example, when someone feels rage, he will often say that he is angry. But anger is something different. Anger is always a simple and straightforward response to a clear and present danger. *Rage is not anger. Rage is a violent form of hate.* This distinction is critical to our understanding of how our emotions function.

When we perceive something as hateful, we are filled with *revulsion*, the desire to get away. A simple example is the nausea we feel when we smell spoiled food. Revulsion is the opposite of desire. If we are not able to escape what we hate, we are filled with a feeling of hurt, the opposite of pleasure. *Hurt* is our experience of enduring what we perceive as bad for us. It can be as simple as being hurt by an unkind remark, or it can be as devastating as losing someone we love.

These are the basic (but not the only) emotions of our lives: the pleasure emotions of love, desire, and pleasure; and their opposites, hate, revulsion, and hurt. They are powerful emotions because their purpose is to keep us alive and well by moving us toward what is good for us and away from what is bad for us *in the concrete, material world.*

We have many words in our language that elucidate different aspects of these basic emotions. Because the world is complex, we experience many shades and intensities of love and hate, of pleasure and hurt. We talk about liking, wanting, craving, satisfaction, enjoyment, sorrow, disgust, and dislike. As we grow and develop, these basic emotions become differentiated through our experience, but *the pleasure emotions remain the tap root of our emotional lives.*

## Hope, Courage, and Anger

There is another kind of emotion. The core of our emotional life is the cycle of love, desire, and pleasure, but most of the time we can't simply reach out and take what we desire. Usually we have to make an *effort* to get what we desire or avoid what we hate.

Fortunately, we come with a set of emotions whose job is *to move us to the effort needed to get what we desire or to avoid what we hate*. These are the *pragmatic emotions* and at their core is *assertiveness*. These emotions are not concerned primarily with responding to what is good or bad for us, with what we desire or hate, but with getting what we desire and avoiding what we hate. In other words, these are the "ways and means" emotions. Like the pleasure emotions, the pragmatic emotions are calls to action, immediate responses to what we experience in the material world.

The first pragmatic emotion is *hope*. When we perceive an obstacle to getting what we desire, hope is the emotion that moves us to overcome that obstacle. Hope is the feeling, "I can do it. I can exert effort and get what I desire." We have many words for hope—optimism, spunk, confidence, determination—but the basic thrust of all of these words is overcoming an obstacle to getting the good we desire.

The second pragmatic emotion is *courage*. When we are faced with something bad or undesirable or with the possibility that something could harm us, courage tells us that we will be able to overcome what is bad or harmful. While hope is the response to an obstacle to getting something good, courage is the response to something bad or to a possible threat. Both hope and courage are assertive emotions, moving us to overcome something.

Like the pleasure emotions, these two pragmatic emotions have opposites, feelings that are the opposite of assertiveness. The opposite of hope is *despair.* To despair means to lose hope. If we perceive something we desire, but we believe that we cannot possibly obtain that good, we feel despair. Then we give up the struggle to get what we desire. The opposite of courage is *fear.* When we believe that we will not be able to escape harm or to overcome it, we feel fear.

There is a fifth pragmatic emotion which, unlike hope and courage, *has no opposite.* This emotion is *anger.* Anger has a very specific function. When we face *immediate danger,* anger protects us from what threatens us. We do not feel anger in the face of a possible threat. *Unless we perceive the threat to be immediately present, we feel either courage or fear.* Then, whether we have felt courage or fear in the face of approaching harm, anger rises up to fight the harm *when it is actually present.*

It is important to realize that *anger is not the same as hate.* Hate in all its forms, including hostility and resentment, is the emotional response to something that we perceive as bad for us but that does not involve an immediate threat. Anger is the response to immediate danger. When the immediate threat is over, anger subsides. The emotion that remains is the feeling that the thing that has aroused our anger is bad, the feeling of hate. Confusion between these two emotions, hate and anger, persists in people's everyday speech. People often speak of being angry with someone, but unless they are in the middle of a threatening situation, what they are feeling is not anger, but hate. So, for instance, if someone says something hurtful to us, we feel anger. If, however, we continue to feel bad after the immediate incident, the emotion we are feeling is hate of what has aroused our anger. *The confusion between anger and hate is at the root of many serious emotional problems.*

# The Pragmatic Emotions Always Serve the Pleasure Emotions

The pleasure emotions and the pragmatic emotions are the basic emotions of human nature. As we grow up and encounter the complexities of the world, our emotions become more finely differentiated as they respond to these complexities. One of the tasks of growing up is to develop the ability to perceive distinctions in what is happening to us and to react to different situations with appropriate emotions and actions. For example, we feel not only fear, but also nervousness, anxiety, and doubt, each of which is a differentiation of the basic emotion of fear. Each of these is a response to a different kind of situation. The feeling of stage fright before giving a speech is different from the fear that we would feel when confronted by a snarling dog. Rehearsing the speech until we are more comfortable would be a more appropriate response to stage fright than running away, while backing away would be an appropriate response to the dog.

*The pleasure emotions are always primary in the life of any human being. Love, desire, and pleasure are the core of our emotional lives. The pragmatic emotions exist to serve and protect the pleasure emotions, to find the ways and means of getting what we desire.*

Christians may become wary at the mention of desire and pleasure. Aren't we supposed to take up our cross? Doesn't this mean denying ourselves what we desire and what gives us pleasure? The problem is that Christians tend to think of desire and pleasure purely in terms of gratification of their physical desires. When the pleasure emotions are functioning properly, the pleasure emotions center on love for others, the desire to be with them, and pleasure in their company. *The primary source of pleasure for human beings lies in their relationships with other human beings and with God.* It is when people feel alone and cut off from these relationships that they turn to unrestrained indulgence in physical pleasures such as sex or food.

Christian teaching has always recognized that love is the center of our being, the root of all that we are. "And now faith, hope, and love abide, these three; and the greatest of these is love" (1 Cor 13:13).

# 2
# When Love Fails

Modern research in child development has found that the truly important thing in a child's life is to feel loved just for being herself, God's own unique creation. If a child feels loved in this way, she is able to love in return. If a child does not feel loved, her emotional development is stunted and distorted. Even though she may grow up to be intelligent, rich, and accomplished, there will be something seriously lacking in her sense of well-being. She will not feel a spontaneous connection to others. Instead, she will feel in some way profoundly and painfully alone.

People who have grown up feeling unloved may blame their parents for the way their parents treated them. The parents, on the other hand, believe that they did the best they could, and they cannot understand how their children can be so resentful and ungrateful after all they have done for them. *But a person who has not herself received spontaneous, unconditional love is not able to give this kind of love to another person in a form that is not flawed.*

A mother who has not felt loved may long with all her heart to love her child in the way she wishes she had been loved. If she has insight into her own emotional suffering, she can often give her child better mothering than she herself received, but often a mother will find that she cannot feel the spontaneous love that she longs to feel for her baby when she most needs to feel it. She may find herself frustrated and overwhelmed by the reality of taking care of a small child. She may have insight into her own difficulty in giving love and still find herself unable to compensate enough for her own shortcomings. Her awareness of her own longing to be loved and to be taken care of can be extremely painful to her. Even though she loves the child, the child senses her pain. *Because a baby cannot understand why her mother feels this way, she experiences her mother's unhappiness as unhappiness with her.* Because her mother cannot enjoy her, she feels that she is not a desirable baby.

Unfortunately, there are many reasons why a child may not feel loved, even if her mother loves her very much. Dr. Stanley I. Greenspan gives an example of how a baby may be sensitive to the world around her in ways that her mother does not understand. She may be sensitive to sound, distressed by noises that others would enjoy. When her mother talks to her, she may experience her mother's voice as too loud. Because she feels overwhelmed by the sound of her mother's voice, the child may withdraw when her mother speaks to her. Her mother, worried that she does not respond, may talk louder, trying to get her attention. The child, feeling her mother's distress, assumes that her mother is not pleased with her, that she must be an unsatisfactory baby.

It is not helpful to blame the parents if a child does not feel loved. A person who has not received the gift of unconditional love cannot give the gift of unconditional love to another without undergoing considerable change. To say this is not to pass judgment on anyone. We live in a world in which it is difficult for love to flourish.

Even if a child does not feel loved, she will still feel love for her mother, desire to be with her, and longing to feel the pleasure of her mother's love for her. If a child does not experience the pleasure of being loved and feeling satisfied, the natural and spontaneous development of her pleasure emotions is stopped in its tracks. *If a child does not experience the satisfaction of her physical needs and of her need to feel loved, her pleasure emotions will continue to demand the kind of concrete material and emotional satisfactions that are appropriate for a small child, the satisfactions that a small child truly does need in order to grow and develop. The pleasure emotions will continue to seek for these satisfactions until they find them, no matter how long a person may live, because the function of the pleasure emotions is to guide the child to what she needs in order to grow into her real self, the self created and given to her by God.* If her childish needs are not satisfied, she will continue, as she grows older, to pursue the satisfaction of her childish needs in ways that we refer to as immature. Her behavior will be immature because her immature needs will still seek the satisfaction they require in order to become mature.

## Creating the Idealized Self

How does the child continue to live and function if her needs have not been met and she does not feel loved? *If a child's pleasure emotions are not satisfied, the child's pragmatic emotions, whose function is to protect and assist the pleasure emotions, will leap into action and take over the job of growing up.* When this happens, the direction of a child's development changes. Normally a child's energy and effort flow naturally into her pleasure emotions. God has given each individual child a particular self—interests, talents, and inclinations. As she grows up, her pleasure emotions lead her to these interests and talents. She may love to draw. She may love to read. She may love to organize all the children in the neighborhood into stickball teams. A child who feels loved just because she is her particular self will develop into the person God created her to be, guided by her pleasure emotions. This is her *real* self.

When the child feels that she is not loved, the pragmatic emotions begin to work with the child's imagination *to overcome the obstacles to finding the love that the child needs.* If I am not loved, the pragmatic emotions reason, I must *make myself lovable.* The pragmatic emotions begin to observe what those around them demand in exchange for approval. Is it obedience? Is it being clever? Is it playing the part of mommy to the child's own mother? The child, ever hopeful and courageous, begins to behave in ways that her parents seem to demand, trying to elicit from them the love she never experiences. *This attempt to earn love can never be successful* because the unconditional love she longs for, the love she needs, can never be earned. It can only be given by an adult who has the capacity and the inclination to love.

## Losing Touch with the Pleasure Emotions

When the pragmatic emotions go to work in an effort to make the child lovable, *the child begins to lose contact with her pleasure emotions.* To feel them would simply be too devastatingly painful. Slowly, over time, the child pays less and less attention to her pleasure emotions, hoping that the pain of her unsatisfied desires will go away. At the same time, the pragmatic emotions, working with the imagination, *begin to construct an ideal child, a mask that the child hopes will please her parents and earn the love she needs.*

The child observes which emotions her parents approve of and slowly begins to stress these emotions while ignoring the emotions her parents disapprove of or dislike. Does a mother smile when her daughter is cheerful and obedient, withholding affection at the first sign of assertiveness? The little girl tries to appear more cheerful than she feels and to suppress her impulses to insist on her own way. Do a boy's parents ignore him when he shows his feelings of helplessness and dependency, paying attention to him only when he screams and demands something? The little boy will soon ignore his own feelings of weakness and needfulness and become even more assertive and demanding.

The girl's cheerful compliance or the boy's loud demands are not the child's real emotions. The child does feel these emotions, but they are not all of what she feels in response to what is happening to her. The girl whose mother smiles only when she is cheerful and obedient hates her mother because her mother is withholding the unconditional love she needs. But the girl will ignore her hate, concentrating instead on exaggerating her love for her mother, love that she does feel, but which is only part of what she feels. Even though the girl tries not to feel hate for her mother, the hate does not go away. The girl simply shoves it out of awareness, striving with hope and courage to present to her mother the emotions she hopes her mother will love.

The boy who receives attention only when he is demanding cannot get rid of his need for love. He is feeling the need for love when he cries and demands attention. He soon learns that showing tenderness, weakness, or dependency is useless. So the boy shoves his feelings of dependency out of awareness because he cannot bear the pain of having his loving overtures rebuffed or ignored. Soon he is aware only of his assertive emotions. If he cannot have his parents' love, he will at least have their attention.

Slowly the child develops *habits of feeling,* consistently presenting to her parents those feelings she thinks they will find acceptable. These habits of feeling seem to her to be the best way both to minimize the terrible pain she feels and to earn what approval she can from her parents. As the child grows up, these habits of feeling become stronger and stronger until the child loses all awareness of her true emotional life. She creates for her parents an *Idealized Self,* an ideal child who feels only what her parents approve of.

# 3
# The Roots of the Idealized Self

The Idealized Self develops when a child feels unloved, when he feels that his real self is not good enough. The child's pragmatic emotions and his imagination work together to create an Idealized Self that he hopes will be *worthy enough to earn* or *strong enough to demand* the love that he needs. This Idealized Self exaggerates the feelings that the child's parents find acceptable. As a result, the child loses any sense of his own desires, thoughts, and interests. His attention becomes focused on his Idealized Self, and he becomes alienated from his pleasure emotions, from his real self. The results of this alienation have been clearly described by Dr. Karen Horney, a European psychoanalyst who practiced in Chicago and New York City.

The child begins to relate to others not from his own desires and emotions, but rather from the desires and emotions that he thinks he *should* have. For example, if the child's parents consistently communicate to him that they want him to be unselfish, the child may try to earn his parents' love by giving away a favorite toy, even though losing the toy is extremely painful. Because he has given the toy away to please his parents, he does not have any real sense of the pleasure of sharing or giving. To him, giving becomes a painful experience motivated by fear of losing his parents' love, not by real satisfaction in sharing. The problem is compounded because the child must deny the pain he feels and must pretend *to himself,* as well as to his parents, that he feels generous.

As he becomes more alienated from his pleasure emotions, his anxiety grows. Because he has no firm sense of who he really is, he must constantly focus on others as he tries to determine what he should do or feel. Because he must try to figure out what his parents want from him, he is never sure where he really stands with them. All of his energy and effort, his hope and courage, go into maintaining and perfecting the Idealized Self.

Underneath the mask of the Idealized Self there lies a chasm of loneliness and anxiety. Children always assume that they are not loved because they are not lovable. They cannot understand that their parents may not be able to love them. A child knows in his deepest self only that he is not loved. He feels cut off from the human race, alone in the universe. This is the reality that the Idealized Self cannot bear to face. The Idealized Self is the defense against feelings of loneliness and misery that seem impossible to bear. Therefore, the Idealized Self cannot allow any breach in its defensive bastion. *The Idealized Self believes that it must be perfect in order to earn love, and it immediately discounts or destroys any perception that it could be less than perfect.*

Deep down, however, the Idealized Self knows that it is far from perfect. It knows that beneath its defensive bastion lies the real self. The Idealized Self loathes the real self because the real self feels the emotions that the Idealized Self cannot bear to face. The Idealized Self is extremely durable because it is determined to survive. It is extremely vulnerable because it is threatened by any experience that challenges its dominance or by any upsurge of the real self's immature desires.

These dangerous emotions and immature desires humiliate the Idealized Self. "How could I be such a miserable, babyish, vulnerable wreck?" the Idealized Self insists. "These longings, these needs, these wishes are not mine." But the pleasure emotions are the root of our being and the Idealized Self cannot eradicate them. No matter what the Idealized Self does to avoid perceiving the real self's desires and needs, those desires and needs remain.

## The Grand and Glorious Idealized Self

In his desperate need to be loved, the child strives to mold himself completely into the image of the Idealized Self, a grand and glorious self, a grandiose self, a self so excellent that the child can believe that this false self *deserves* to receive all the love that the child's real self so desperately needs. The child understands in his deepest self that all human beings were created to receive unconditional love, but he cannot imagine what it would be like to receive it. Since he cannot imagine unconditional love, he must insist to himself that he is good enough to earn some semblance of love. In this way, the child's very real needs turn in his own mind into *demands* and *claims* based not on his needs, but on the worthiness of the Idealized Self. Because his needs are so real and desperate, the child must see himself as still greater and grander in order to support the hope that he is worthy to have his needs met.

Because the Idealized Self bases its claim to love on its own excellence, it must begin to *exaggerate its positive qualities.* The Idealized Self then presents these positive qualities to the outside world as proof that it is worthy to have its claims met. This exaggeration of positive qualities develops into *pride* in these qualities. Because this pride is based on exaggerated claims of excellence and not on any actual sense of accomplishing what the real self wants to accomplish, this pride is a false pride. It has no foundation in reality. Instead, it is based on the illusion of a grandiose self built up in response to the parents' failure to accept the real self.

The child may still have some awareness of his real self, but more and more *he comes to experience his real self as an enemy, as something that he must destroy in order to create the ideal child.* In fact, the false pride hides a pool of contempt and disdain for his real self. In Chapter 1, we pointed out that the opposite of love is hate. We experience what we hate as bad or undesirable. If a child is not loved, he experiences himself as undesirable, as bad, as hated. He learns to hate his real self, and *he uses this hate to try to eradicate the "bad" real self so that he can become the Idealized Self he longs to be.*

The child measures his real self by the standard of the Idealized Self. Since the Idealized Self is a false self with no foundation in the child's own pleasure emotions, the child's energies must continually flow into maintaining the false self and into eliminating the parts of himself that he hates. This self-hate, this contempt for his real self, is so painful that he focuses his attention even more on the Idealized Self, and he becomes identified in his own mind with the Idealized Self. Because the Idealized Self is not based on the full reality of who he is, the child will fail again and again to live up to his Idealized Self. When he fails, he will feel even more hate for his real self. Thus the child is caught in a seesaw between hope that he really can become his Idealized Self and the painful realization that the real self, which he hates so much, is still there.

Whenever the child becomes aware of his real self in its weakness, his false pride is hurt. He experiences either shame or humiliation, two forms of self-hate. A child feels *shame* when he perceives the real self that he hates so much. He feels *humiliation* when he thinks that *others* have seen his hated real self.

Any wound to his false pride brings a wave of self-hate. Because the self-hate is so terribly painful, his pragmatic emotions must leap into action to protect him from such suffering. The child then feels a secondary reaction, a reaction that covers up the self-hate. *This secondary reaction is usually either rage or fear.* The child can experience this secondary reaction in a wide range of intensities. He may experience rage as irritation, as dislike, or as murderous rage. He may experience fear as anxiety, as nervousness, or as terror.

Whatever the intensity of the secondary reaction, it becomes *automatic*. The child often will not experience self-hate at all. He will be aware only of his irritation with the situation or of his nervousness with people. As the child grows up, the secondary reaction becomes deeply embedded in the fabric of the Idealized Self.

## How Self-Hate Shows Itself

As the child grows up, the expressions of his self-hate multiply. First, he makes enormous demands on himself. The Idealized Self creates a system of what Dr. Horney calls the *shoulds,* expectations that the child *must* live up to in order to fend off the self-hate. These *shoulds* are absolute. The child should be perfectly loving, helpful, kind, understanding, and unselfish. Or he should be perfectly strong, self-reliant, aggressive, and successful. Any failure to live up to these standards brings a wave of self-hate.

We can see these *shoulds* operating in many adults. People may believe that they must say "yes" to every request to serve, whether or not they have the time and energy to do so. They may believe that they must have the perfect solution for every problem that arises and an absolutely helpful suggestion for every friend's woes. They may believe that they must love everyone and never judge anyone, even to the point of entrusting their life savings to a "Christian Investment Fund," whether or not the fund seems reliable. They may believe that to have anything for themselves would be selfish. The problem here is not with loving or serving, but with the absolute demands that people make on themselves in the futile attempt to fend off self-hate.

A second expression of self-hate is *self-accusation*. Many people feel guilty not for doing something wrong, but for not being good enough. Even if they do their best to live up to the *shoulds* that the Idealized Self has created, they attack themselves on the grounds that their motives are not pure. Yes, they did canvass the neighborhood for the American Cancer Society, but they did it only to feel important. Or, if they externalize this criticism of themselves, they may feel that others see the bad motives that really underlie their service.

Along with self-accusation goes *self-contempt*. Many people do not value their own work and time. Yes, they spent the weekend baking cookies for the third grade when they were exhausted from setting up for the Business Women's Banquet, but the time and effort don't really count. To silence their own self-contempt, these people need others' approval and praise for their efforts. They feel disappointed if people do not notice how much they do.

*Self-frustration* is another common expression of self-hate that takes on a mask of nobility. Self-discipline becomes another word for self-abuse when that discipline does not admit any limits. There are some Christians, for example, who eat no meat or dairy products during Lent, even if they become ill or grow so irritable that their families beg them to have a hamburger. This kind of false discipline demands perfection, taking no account of a person's age, health, or emotional problems. The Idealized Self insists that a modified fast wouldn't be enough.

Self-hate can also take the form of *procrastination*. A person may fail to do something he knows he needs to do and then berate himself for failing to do it. Self-hate can take the form of *hypochondria*, a continual fear that some terrible disease will strike. Some people deprive themselves, wearing shoes after they have worn out or not wearing a jacket when it is cold. They may fail to take care of themselves, not exercising or getting enough sleep. They may feel that they don't deserve to enjoy anything. All of these, even though they masquerade as virtues, are forms of self-hate. Finally, self-hate can culminate in truly self-destructive behavior such as abusing drugs or engaging in promiscuous sex. It can take the form of actually hurting oneself, accidentally spilling boiling water on one's hand or insisting on passing a truck on a blind curve.

## How Self-Hate Hides Itself

All these are forms of self-hate. But the Idealized Self cannot bear to be aware of this self-destructive behavior, so the Idealized Self convinces itself that these behaviors are really virtues. Working oneself to exhaustion is ordinary unselfishness. Strict fasting is a religious duty. Passing a truck on a blind curve is daring. The *compulsive* nature of these behaviors is the indication that they are forms of self-hate rather than the virtues they pretend to be. For example, a person's Idealized Self may demand that he volunteer for any committee that needs new members. "It's just like there's a magnet in my hand," one woman said. "When someone asks for volunteers, no matter what I want to do, an electrical current goes on in the ceiling and yanks my hand up."

If a person tries to ignore the Idealized Self's demands, the price is a wave of self-hate. Taking care of oneself, the Idealized Self whispers, is self-indulgence. Refusing to chair the United Way is laziness. What would happen if everyone did just what they wanted? A person in the grip of the Idealized Self does not serve others out of a deeply felt desire to serve, but rather out of a desire to avoid the self-hate he feels if he does not serve.

The Idealized Self continues to insist that the real self does not feel the emotions that the Idealized Self finds unacceptable. What does the Idealized Self do with these stubborn, unacceptable emotions? Since it cannot admit that the real self feels these emotions, the Idealized Self *projects them outward* and sees the emotions in someone else.

The Idealized Self can project the real self's unacceptable emotions onto other people in different ways. *Some people insist that they do not feel the bad emotions. It is other people who feel these emotions.* This form of projection insists that other people are selfish, greedy, lazy, or have immoral desires. These other people must be either corrected or shunned. The Idealized Self is outraged at other people's bad emotions and bad behavior. How, it asks, could other people do such things? How could they feel that way? How could they believe those things? By focusing its attention on others, the Idealized Self can avoid noticing that what it most dislikes in others is just what it dislikes most in its own real self.

Another way in which the Idealized Self projects unacceptable emotions outward is to insist that *other people see the unacceptable emotions that the real self feels.* The Idealized Self is sure that other people see how selfish, greedy, bad, or lazy the real self is. Others see the real self's every fault and judge it harshly. Other people hate him. He doesn't hate himself. The Idealized Self can then insist that he redouble his efforts to please others and to feel only acceptable feelings.

## The Idealized Self and Religion

One of the primary charges leveled against religious people today is that they are hypocrites. *What people see as the hypocrite is really the face of the Idealized Self.* For example, when children hear their parents talking about love, but they do not experience their parents as loving them, they may see their parents as hypocritical. When parents insist that they feel one thing but their children experience them as feeling something else, the children may call them hypocrites. The parents cannot understand what their children are talking about. Surely their children can see that they feel loving, patient, and kind. They experience themselves that way. Why don't their children see them that way?

Children of religious parents may turn away from their parents' religion. Because their parents have rejected their emotions, they look elsewhere for love and acceptance, certain that the rejection they have experienced is an integral part of that religion.

When young people leave religious institutions, charging their members with hypocrisy, they usually take with them their own hostility, resentment, bitterness, and their own need for love. They keep the same destructive emotional patterns and fill them with new content. We see young people who exchange their parents' faith for faith in drugs or sexual acting out. Others turn vegetarianism, or peace, or ecology into a religion. The problem is not vegetarianism or a concern for the natural world, but rather the destructive emotional patterns that young people can bring to their support of these causes. They often end up feeling all the things they have most hated in their parents and in their parents' faith— condemnation of others' behavior, hostility, judgment of others who do not agree with them—in the service of their own beliefs. Religion may become an arena for the battle between young people and their parents, with hostility and resentment on all sides.

Controversial issues may also become a battleground for Idealized Selves, people on each side of an issue convinced that it is those on the other side who are causing all of the problems. Each Idealized Self projects its own emotions onto its opponents. The Idealized Self usually cannot see another's point of view and is often certain that anyone who holds another view must be blind or evil. It stigmatizes and caricatures its opponents' concerns. Whatever truth may exist on either side of an issue is lost in emotional rancor.

# When the Mask of the Idealized Self Slips

When the Idealized Self tries to banish unacceptable emotions, these emotions are free to roam out of control, tucked out of sight and projected outward. Then a person can see his own hostility as justified by others' bad behavior. He is sure that his rage is caused by others' faults or false beliefs. He believes that others don't appreciate all that he does.

But even as he projects his unacceptable emotions onto others and insists that he truly is his Idealized Self, he knows deep down that he is not really that Idealized Self. He knows that there are emotions inside him that he fears and is ashamed of. He cannot bear to be aware of them. But when he fails to perform as grandly as his Idealized Self demands that he perform, when he sees something that his real self still longs for, when he feels rejected, or when he wakes up at three in the morning in a cold sweat, he knows that the Idealized Self is a mask, and he despises himself. He is terrified of these feelings. At these times, he may resolve to change. But the next morning, as he steps into the life that his Idealized Self has created, the Idealized Self takes over again. He forgets the resolve to change until the next time these terrible feelings strike.

While all Idealized Selves share certain basic characteristics— the *shoulds,* the demand for perfection, the self-hate, the inability to know what the real self feels or desires—the shape that the Idealized Self takes depends on a child's inborn temperament and on the culture he lives in. The child begins to stress certain emotions and to ignore others in response to the demands that those around him make. As the child grows up, *he may comply with these demands or he may struggle against them.* For example, he may give his favorite Christmas present to charity or he may rebel against his parents' demands that he be unselfish by stealing. In either case, he does not experience what he really wants. Instead, he reacts to his parents' demands, *whether he reacts by complying or by rebelling.*

As the child grows into adulthood, his identification with the grand and glorious Idealized Self comes into conflict with the realization that he will never really be able to live up to the demands of the Idealized Self. The conflict between these two sets of emotions tears the child apart, and he begins to ignore one or the other of them. A child's inborn temperament, his parents' demands, whether the child complies with or rebels against these demands, whether he identifies with the Idealized Self or with his realization that he can never be his Idealized Self—all these factors shape the different forms that the Idealized Self can take.

# 4
# The Branches of the Idealized Self

As the child's Idealized Self battles with her real self, she *struggles desperately to create some unified sense of self.* Slowly the child develops particular patterns of dealing with the world. These patterns are the *defenses* that she uses to cope with her parents' expectations and to avoid feeling her terrible pain. These patterns serve the child well as she deals with her parents, but they can be ineffective when she uses them to deal with the world outside her home. Such a pattern, commonly called a *neurosis,* persists, becoming more elaborate and fixed as the child grows up. By the time she has become an adult, she regularly relies on her usual defenses, and she experiences herself as being a particular kind of person. The emotions she learned to focus on as a child influence the kind of self she experiences herself as being. In this chapter we describe the basic patterns of defense, the patterns of neurosis, that the Idealized Self tends to take. The exact form that an Idealized Self takes depends on the culture in which a child lives. The patterns we describe here are common in American culture.

When a person sees herself in one of these descriptions, when she recognizes some aspect of herself that she does not like, her first impulse is often to attack herself. But if someone does not feel well, she goes to a doctor to find the cause of the problem. The doctor makes a diagnosis in order to determine what he needs to do to help the patient. The doctor's purpose in making the diagnosis is not to accuse the patient of being ill or to condemn her for having cancer or diabetes. Our purpose in describing the patterns of the Idealized Self is not to accuse anyone, nor is it to give anyone ammunition to use in condemning someone else. We recommend that the reader be self-critical but not self-condemnatory. Criticism is not the same thing as condemnation, blame, or finding fault. Criticism means saying, "I think it would work better if you did it another way." Each of these patterns grows out of a child's need to deal with devastating pain and sorrow. The Idealized Self develops when a child does not feel loved, and when a child does not feel loved, she *has no choice* but to deal with the pain in the best way she can.

## The Three Basic Patterns of Neurosis

Karen Horney describes *three basic patterns of neurosis* that can develop as a child grows into adulthood. In the first pattern, which we call the *self-affirming neurosis,* the person *identifies with and tries to affirm the strong and capable Idealized Self.* Many books have been written encouraging people to affirm themselves, but self-affirmation does not work. A person cannot effectively affirm herself. Although a person can do much to help herself in her emotional development, she must receive love from another. God created human beings to live together. Our need to love and be loved is the glue that holds us together. It is popular in some circles to speak of creating one's own self. The truth is that we receive our self as a gift from God and from other human beings when we are loved just for who we are. If there is no one in our life who loves us for who we are, we can turn to God to receive this love. And when we turn to God *in the humility of our real self,* the God who loves us will often set us among those who can be the human face of his love for us.

Self-affirmation also does not work because a person usually affirms not her real self, but her Idealized Self. When a person is in the grip of the Idealized Self, it is difficult for her to see, let alone to affirm, her real self. Her real self seems to her to be the enemy. Few books on self-affirmation advise people to affirm the miserable, hostile, fearful part of themselves that they hate most. But until we recognize and love the real self, we cannot become the person we were created to be.

In the second basic pattern of neurosis, which we call the *self-denying neurosis*, the person *identifies neither with her real self nor with the Idealized Self, but with the hate that her Idealized Self feels for her real self.* She believes that her parents found her unlovable and she identifies with this judgment. Her reaction to feeling unlovable is to demonstrate how much she loves others.

In the third basic pattern, which we call the *paralyzed neurosis*, the person has been *overwhelmed by her internal conflicts.* Because her only goal is to survive without activating the painful conflict between her real self and her Idealized Self, she wants nothing and tries to accomplish nothing. She withdraws from the world and limits herself to doing only what she needs to do to survive. In some way, this is the most serious neurosis, since the person is unaware of most of her own emotions.

# The Self-Affirming Neurosis

A person with a self-affirming neurosis identifies with his Idealized Self. He has learned to focus on his pragmatic emotions, his hope and courage, in an effort to make the Idealized Self a reality. He is assertive and determined to overcome any obstacle, whether within himself or in the world around him. His Idealized Self ruthlessly shoves all feelings of need or weakness out of awareness because they are too painful and the Idealized Self despises them. Terrified of feeling helpless, he is driven by the ambition to prove to himself and to everyone else that he really is his Idealized Self. Karen Horney calls this the defense of moving against people.

Identification with the Idealized Self can take one of three forms, depending on which aspect of the Idealized Self a person identifies with.

## The Grandiose Idealized Self

The *grandiose Idealized Self identifies with a great mission or calling,* and such a person appears to truly believe in his own greatness as an advocate of that mission. The mission can take many forms: reforming the government, finding a new source of renewable energy, or writing the great American novel. Because he serves such a noble cause, he feels that there is nothing that he is not entitled to and nothing that he cannot do. He appears never to doubt himself. He loves to include others in his mission, to let them share in his greatness. He can laugh when others joke about him—as long as the joke is about some endearing quirk or foible. But if anyone should seriously question what he is doing, he becomes furious. He cannot see how anyone could doubt the importance of what he is trying to accomplish, and he attempts to surround himself with people who can really understand him. He has no true friends. Many experience him as unscrupulous, and he can't understand why. In his own eyes, his great mission justifies whatever he thinks he must do to accomplish it. When he is called to account for any bad behavior, he is truly baffled.

## The Perfectionistic Idealized Self

The *perfectionistic Idealized Self identifies with its own high standards.* This person knows what is right, and he looks down on others who do not share these standards. Just knowing what is right makes him superior. He does try to live up to the standards, but his Idealized Self will not allow him to see his own failures. He intends to be moral and hardworking and he "reckons these intentions unto himself as righteousness." Often, he believes that knowing what is right entitles him to what he calls "fair treatment." He believes that his own success and prosperity have come to him by right of his high standards and hard work, and if he doesn't get what he expects, he is sure that it isn't fair. His success is proof of his virtue. By contrast, he is sure that anyone who does not achieve success has failed because he deserves to fail. People who fail don't work hard enough. They don't have the right values. They don't really try. The perfectionist is certain that no one ever gave him anything. He earned it all by himself. Why should he give anything to anyone if they don't have the gumption to work for it themselves?

## *The Arrogant Idealized Self*

The *arrogant Idealized Self identifies with its accomplishments.* This person is extremely competitive. He cannot bear for anyone to be richer, more powerful, or more intelligent than he is. Since he prides himself on his ability to see through others' pretended accomplishments, he is quite certain that he is simply being honest and forthright when he makes hostile remarks to others. His accomplishments entitle him to speak his mind. He intimidates others and believes that he is entitled to have whatever he wants with a total disregard for what others might feel or need. He is prone to violent rages, but he is sure that he doesn't get mad, he gets even. He justifies his own hostility by exaggerating other people's hostility and dishonesty, and he sees himself as an expert in exposing hypocrisy in others. He is certain that an evil motive really lurks behind every good deed. No one really feels kindness or love, as far as he is concerned. It's all about accomplishment.

*A person who identifies with his Idealized Self externalizes his self-hate. He hates and despises in others what he cannot bear to see in himself.* Since he denies his own weakness and need for love, he has nothing but contempt for those who are weak and needful. Since he identifies with his need to be right, he lives in a castle of self-righteousness and loathes those who do not share his values. He is certain that he is entitled to impose his standards on others and becomes punitive when others don't or won't live up to those standards. He has no sympathy for anyone, not even for himself. He cannot believe that anyone else's joy is real, and he enjoys exposing the phoniness behind any apparent goodness.

## The Self-Denying Neurosis

The person with a *self-denying neurosis* identifies not with her strong, righteous Idealized Self, but with her parents' feeling that she is unlovable. *She is profoundly aware of her inability to live up to the Idealized Self's absolute standards, and she hates herself for it.* She focuses her attention on her feelings of love for others, just as she focused on her feelings of love for her parents. She cannot bear to recognize the rage and hostility that she really feels. Because she hates herself and because she focuses on earning love by pleasing and serving others, her Idealized Self demands that she must never feel superior to anyone else. This is often mistaken for humility. But this is not true humility because such a person cannot bear to look at herself as she really is. One sign that this is not true humility is that she is so proud of being humble.

Such a person feels devastated by her failure to live up to the *shoulds* that the Idealized Self imposes on her. She should be perfectly loving, perfectly understanding, perfectly unselfish, perfectly helpful, generous, and humble. Since she cannot be perfect, she does not deserve anything. She has no rights. Any desire she might have is a sign of selfishness. She can't enjoy anything unless others enjoy it, too. Her salvation is in taking care of others, in helping others, in rescuing others. She cannot be alone, and only others give meaning to her life. Karen Horney calls this the defense of moving toward people.

For this person, love is everything, and she sees herself as totally loving and devoted. She will exhaust herself trying to love and serve those whose love and approval she longs for. She is likely to become involved with people who are grandiose, righteous, or arrogant since these people seem so certain of who they are and often respond positively, at least for a while, to the devotion that the selfless person longs to give.

What such a person's Idealized Self will not let her see, however, is what she demands in return for such selflessness. In return for her service to others, she demands that others provide her with attention, approval, gratitude, sympathy, and love. When she does not receive the attention and approval she is certain she deserves, her underlying rage and hostility take the form of feeling abused and taken advantage of. This feeling of being abused becomes the basis of her secret picture of herself as a martyr. She uses her sense of being abused to accuse others in her own mind. If only they knew what she has gone through for them. Someday they will understand and appreciate it. The hostility that she really feels may take the form of physical illness or depression.

The person with a self-denying neurosis also projects onto others the feelings that she cannot acknowledge in herself. Instead of seeing other people as feeling the bad feelings, a self-denying person sees others as feeling those unacknowledged feelings toward her. While a person with a self-affirming neurosis may see others as lazy, sinful, or weak, a person with a self-denying neurosis believes that other people see her as lazy, sinful, or weak.

Then she must try even harder to please them and to earn their approval.

# The Paralyzed Neurosis

The person with a *paralyzed neurosis has simply given up the struggle to deal with his internal conflicts.* He does not identify with his Idealized Self. Neither does he feel any hope of earning love by denying himself or pleasing others. As he grew up, those around him made such overwhelming and conflicting demands on him that he could find no way to deal with them, and he has come to the conclusion that the only way to survive is to want nothing, to do nothing, to need nothing. To this person, the ultimate goal is freedom. This does not mean freedom from external oppression, but rather freedom from the terrible conflicts that lie outside his awareness. Because so many things in the world around him can arouse these conflicts, he avoids everything. All he wants is to be left alone. He may feel some affection toward others, but he does not allow this to go beyond his own private experience. He may find something interesting or pleasurable, but he cannot allow this to develop into an actual desire for anything. He feels that it is best to make do with whatever life gives him. To actually desire anything would be to activate the overwhelming feelings of fear, despair, and rage that fill him.

Because he externalizes his *shoulds,* he experiences the demands that the Idealized Self makes on himself as coming from other people. As a result, he is extremely sensitive to what he perceives as pressure from others. He cannot stand to have anyone expect him to do or to be anything. He may temporarily give in to what someone else demands of him. After all, he wants above all to avoid conflict. But when he feels too much pressure, he will run away from the situation. He values his freedom above everything else, and he defines freedom as being free from anything that others might expect of him. To admit that he longs to be loved would be to bring up his overwhelming feelings of fear, despair, and rage. He feels that it is better to be alone. Karen Horney calls this the defense of moving away from people. This defense is often at the root of substance abuse, addiction, and depression.

## Why We Don't Change

*These three sets of defenses do not exist unalloyed.* Some individuals tend to switch from one set of defenses to another at intervals, sometimes at shorter intervals and sometimes at longer intervals.

The tragedy of all of these neuroses is that they resemble real virtues. The self-affirming neurotic may be highly successful in the service of a noble cause—as an environmentalist, a physician, a politician. The self-denying neurotic is the backbone of many organizations, serving on numerous committees and doing what needs to be done. The paralyzed neurotic may renounce the world, giving up all he has and going off by himself to seek truth.

What separates these neuroses from true virtues are the deep emotional conflicts that lie outside the person's awareness and lead to actions that are outside of her control. The person who suffers from any of these neuroses is not the person she thinks she is. She finds herself doing things that she can't understand and is ashamed of, but she can't seem to stop doing them. *It is these deep emotional conflicts that lie at the root of her inability to change.* When one of these conflicts is triggered by something—something she may not even be aware of at the time—the neurotic finds herself smoking, eating, shopping, acting out sexually, drinking, or screaming at her children. In fact, she uses the drinking, smoking, or shopping to keep these conflicts outside of her awareness. In that second just before she takes a drink, lights a cigarette, or buys the new dress she doesn't need, she knows that she feels weak and unloved. Or she knows that she is full of murderous rage. But she cannot bear to acknowledge these emotions.

When this happens, many people redouble their efforts to banish the emotions that they hate and fear in themselves. After all, they think, what would happen if they let that rage out? Look at the people who have rammed someone's car, or shot people, or beat their children. Better, they think, to get a grip on the rage and shove it firmly out of sight.

Others wake up at three in the morning with the awareness that they are not the paragons of virtue that they want others to believe they are. They know that certain habits trip them up again and again. They know that they are ashamed. They know that they are afraid and weak. They fear that they could go to pieces. Much better to pull themselves together and get on with their lives.

There are times when each of these people recognizes that she is not what she hopes to be. She glimpses for a moment the emotions that she wishes she did not have. Over and over she turns to "will power" in order to overcome habits and emotions that she is ashamed of. But will power fails again and again. What can she do?

Our emotions are an important and powerful part of who we are. But our emotions are not all of who we are. We have two other abilities—our reason and our will. These abilities can help us to guide our emotions, but we need to learn how to use them. Our modern idea of will power does not work. *Unless we understand how our reason and our will really work, we can end up doing grave harm to ourselves and to others.* When we understand our reason and our will, we can understand how to overcome the Idealized Self, free ourselves from our painful feelings and the habits we hate, and find the self we were created to be.

# 5
# Following Your Desires

We were created to love and to desire. Love and desire lead us to what is good for us. Popular books advise us to follow our bliss or follow our hearts, and this is good advice. But *when we are in the grip of the Idealized Self, it is very difficult for us to know what we truly desire.*

A child who does not feel loved ceases to pay attention to what he desires and instead *takes over other people's desires and turns them into his own.* As he grows up, these false desires take center stage in his life. At some point he may rebel against the false desires. Many people have awakened one morning realizing that they have spent their lives doing what someone else wanted them to do. They have then abandoned what they saw as a false life to follow their own desires.

*The problem is that while people can abandon the external trappings of the false self, they cannot escape from the Idealized Self* because the real self is still inaccessible to them. The Idealized Self creates a new great and glorious self—a poet, an explorer, an actor, or the boss's boss—and, while the external life may change, the patterns of feeling and behavior do not change. They may seem to change, but *they often change only by switching from one form of the Idealized Self to another.* So, for instance, a woman who has denied her own desires in order to serve her husband's dreams may suddenly feel that she has wasted her life. At this point, *she may switch from a self-denying neurosis to a self-affirming neurosis.* Instead of denying her self, she begins to affirm a grand

and glorious self that longs to be a lawyer, a missionary, a college professor, or simply rich.

*If she does not pay attention to the emotions that she despises in herself—her loneliness, her fear, her rage—she comes no closer to her real self by becoming a lawyer than she did by denying herself for her husband.* She is still in the grip of the Idealized Self and its false desires. *Many people who say that they want to change really mean that they want a new, improved Idealized Self.*

If we were going to renovate an old house, we would not begin with paint and wallpaper. First we would check the foundation, the plumbing, and the wiring. The same thing applies to ourselves. If we are going to change, we have to treat the underlying causes of our suffering, going beneath the cosmetic changes that the Idealized Self wants to make. If we want to change, we have to deal with our real self, the foundation of who we are.

Like renovating a house, renovating ourselves takes time, and the improvements do not become obvious all at once. For a long time things may look worse than they did before we began.

As we change, we must do two things at once. *First we must face the Idealized Self's destructive patterns of behavior, remaining constantly aware of these patterns.* We must understand the tactics and defenses of the Idealized Self if we are going to free ourselves from them. *At the same time, we must also allow our pleasure emotions to grow and develop.* How can we go about doing this?

## Knowing and Desiring

We may have tried to solve our emotional problems by using will power or self-control and been defeated again and again by our own emotions. The idea of "will power" involves a serious misunderstanding of what the will is and how it works. It is the Idealized Self that promotes the idea of "will power." If we are really going to change, we have to go about changing in a different way.

We have to begin with our understanding of how human beings work. People often think of emotions as blind forces. If we operate within a framework that sees human behavior as driven by forces, then we can see the will only as one force within us that we use to control other forces called emotions. *This view of human nature as a bundle of competing forces stands in the way of change.*

Human beings are not defined by external or internal forces, but rather by their human *abilities.* We have the abilities to know the material world and to take action within it. The abilities that do this are our senses and our emotions. We share these two abilities with plants and animals. Both plants and animals sense what is happening around them and take action in response to what they sense. For example, as the day progresses, plants turn in order to receive the optimum amount of sun.

Human beings do not live only in the material world as plants and animals do. We also live in the spiritual world, and because we live in the spiritual world, we have abilities that allow us to function in the spiritual world. These abilities are our *intellect* and our *will.*

Our intellect is able to do more than sense the material world and respond to it. Our intellect is able to *understand* the material world. We do more than sense that an apple is falling from a tree and either get out of the way or catch the apple and eat it. We can think about gravity, nutrition, and the occupational safety of apple pickers.

Just as the senses perceive the material world, the intellect perceives the reality beyond the material world, realities such as justice and health. But the senses never merely perceive. When human beings perceive something, perception moves them to action, and this movement to action is called an emotion. Similarly, when the intellect perceives something, that perception also moves it to action. *The movement to action in the spiritual world is called the will. The will is the spiritual analog of the emotions.* The fundamental emotions are love, desire, and pleasure. *The fundamental actions of the will are love, desire, and joy. The fundamental action of the intellect is to see what is good. The fundamental action of the will is to love what is good.*

But our perceptions of the spiritual world are dim. Since there are many conflicting goods, what is good in a given situation is not always obvious. We human beings face a myriad of choices. The desires and pleasures of the material world are indeed good. But they are often out of sync with the desires and joys of the spiritual world. Unfortunately, our ability to perceive what is truly good for us is limited. Our intellect, our ability to perceive the spiritual world and its relationship to the material world, is darkened. Our will, our ability to love the good in both the material and spiritual worlds, finds itself pulled by every passing good.

It is critical that we learn how to love each good properly, that is, in an ordered fashion. Food is good, but if we love food more than anything else, that is not good. Friendship is good, but if our friends pressure us into stealing a car, that is not good. Food and friendship are not bad. Only when food and friendship do not take their proper places in our lives can they be bad for us. We have to learn to love each good in the right way.

This is where our intellect and will come into play. Our intellect and our will allow us to have a deeper understanding of reality, and this allows us to change. But if the intellect and will are going to do their jobs, *we have to understand how they really work.* In the next three chapters we will discuss the intellect, the will, and how all of our human abilities can work together in a way that helps us to change.

# 6
# A Way of Understanding

In Genesis, God created human beings from the dust of the earth, from the same stuff as the animals. Then God added something else. He breathed his own spirit into Adam and Eve, making them in his own image and likeness. Part of them was dust, part was spirit. In addition to the emotions that we share with the animals, we have an intellect, a unique way of perceiving the world that animals do not share.

In addition to knowing the material world in a concrete way, we have the ability to grasp or apprehend an object of thought. This is analogous to what animals do, but it is not the same. The intellect allows us to make observations and decisions not just about things, but about kinds of things, what philosophers call abstract knowledge. We can talk about something called gravity, not just know that things fall downward when they are dropped. These abstractions—ideas like gravity, economics, and mercy—include and grow out of our experiences of the material world, but they go beyond them.

*The intellect moves us to connect with the world in the same way that the emotions move us to connect with the material world.* Whenever we perceive something good, we want to become one with it, and the intellect becomes one with things by *knowing* them. When we find something interesting, this is a desire to know. *The desire to know is not separate from our emotions.* We love to know things. We feel pleasure when we know things, whether it is what the neighbors are really up to or why the sky is blue. When a child asks "why," she is experiencing the pleasure of knowing and understanding. As a child grows up, her intellect develops out of and is dependent upon her senses and her emotions. Likewise, as a child grows up, *her senses and emotions need to learn to be guided by her intellect.*

## How the Intellect Works

The intellect functions in two different modes. First of all, we have a *theoretical intellect* that discriminates between what is true and what is false. This aspect of our intellect looks at things in themselves, not just in relation to what we desire, and it sees what they are like in themselves and how they fit together. When we want to know what something is like, we are using our theoretical intellect. For instance, a child may be fascinated by beetles. She may learn everything she can about them, not because she wants to eat them, or train them to perform in a circus, or because she wants to earn a living as an entomologist, but just because she wants to know about them. She wants to know their habits and how all the different beetles look. Is it true that all beetles are green? Is it true that beetles spring spontaneously out of balls of dung as the ancient Egyptians thought they did? Is it true that some bugs that look like beetles are not really beetles? This is a way of knowing that only human beings have.

The second mode of knowing is concerned with things as they relate to our own desires and with what we should best do in a given situation, how to behave in the here and now. This kind of knowing is about action. It is called the *practical intellect,* and it is this part of the intellect that we use all the time. The store clerk gave me an extra dollar in change. Should I tell her and give it back? I have an important meeting on the afternoon of my daughter's birthday party. Which gathering should I attend? My neighbor just invited me over for a drink while her husband is out of town and my wife is at a meeting. Should I go?

Whenever we have a question about what would be the best action to take, we are using the practical intellect. Notice that we said the best action. Whenever we ask ourselves what we should do, we are recognizing that there are conflicting good things we desire that lead to different actions. *Each of these goods is, at some level, really good.* At a purely sense level, an affair with a neighbor might bring immediate pleasure. At a level we can understand with our intellect, the affair would bring harm. It is in the conflict between these two levels of understanding, the material level and the abstract or broader level, that we experience the question of what we *should* do.

When we talk about "abstract" thinking, we do not mean theoretical physics. We are referring to a particularly human way of understanding that involves a wider context and a deeper understanding. The sequence of emotions—love, desire, joy—is kicked off by the perception of something good. In the emotions of animals, perception is tied concretely to action. In human beings, *there is a break in the direct tie between perception and action.* This is because human beings are able to understand a greater number, a higher level, of relationships among things in the world.

For example, I may be crossing the desert suffering from terrible thirst and see a water hole ahead, but if there is a sign next to the water hole that says, "This water is poisoned," I will at least hesitate before I drink the water. The process that takes place as I hesitate is carried out by the intellect, and it is this process of comparing different levels of knowledge—the desire for the water that would quench my thirst and the understanding that the water might harm me—that separates us from the animals. Thirst is concrete. The information on the sign is abstract.

Here we can see the interaction of the theoretical and practical aspects of the intellect. The theoretical intellect is concerned with whether or not what the sign says is true. If the side of the water hole were littered with the bones of animals, I might suspect that the statement was true. The practical intellect is concerned with how the truth of that statement relates to my desire for water. If I were walking across a golf course on a hot day after drinking a lemonade and I saw a sign beside a pond that said that the water was poisoned, I might be curious about whether the statement was true (theoretical intellect), but my practical intellect would be engaged in a very different way than it would be in the middle of a desert.

## Knowing What Is Good for Us

Since the practical intellect is concerned with the best action to take in a given situation, the practical intellect is concerned with what is moral, with what it is good and bad for us to do. Our intellect and our senses present us with information on various things that might be good for us. Morality has to do with the actions we take in response to this information.

Knowing what is good for one person, or for many people, is not always easy. We not only have to know what is good for people in general, we need to know the particular situation, the truth about what is really going on in the circumstances. The intellect does not only need to know what principle to apply in a given situation. (Do not steal.) It also needs to know the exact situation in order to understand how to apply the principle. (Can a four-year-old who takes another child's toy be said to be stealing and be put in jail for it?) It is the job of the intellect to determine the truth as well as it can and to determine on the basis of that truth what the best action would be.

The intellect's ability to understand, like everything else human, is limited. It is difficult for us to determine what the truth is. We cannot just see what is true or not true, what is good or not good. We make mistakes. That is why the intellect has a way of operating, a process that it goes through to bring us as close as possible to the truth. The three steps of this process are called *conception, judgment,* and *reasoning.*

## The Intuitive Intellect

In the process of conception we know things as they are, similar to the way we perceive things with our senses. We know what color is. We know that there are things and that we can give them names. This way of knowing is also referred to as the *intuitive intellect,* because it is with this part of the intellect that *we just know things without reasoning about them.* Some people would deny that we can know anything as it is, but they deny this with their theoretical intellects and continue to behave every day as if they know things as they are—red, heavy, tasty, desirable, large. We are born with part of this way of knowing. For instance, all cultures classify colors in similar patterns. Children learn to speak a language. We are born knowing what facial expressions mean. People in every known human culture can tell whether someone is angry or happy by reading his facial expression. Try to imagine a culture in which someone turned red in the face and smashed a chair against the wall as a way of extending a friendly invitation to dinner.

In addition to these inborn abilities, however, we also learn and develop. As we do, we incorporate what we learn into our understanding so that as each separate thing presents itself to us, we don't have to stop and figure out what it is all over again. When we see a tall, thin thing, brown on the bottom with green fluffy stuff on top, we know it is a tree. We don't have to stop and run through a list of possible categories and reason our way to a definition.

Included in the intuitive intellect is our understanding of things that we have learned both emotionally and intellectually. *Our intellectual categories grow out of our emotional categories.* For example, young children respond strongly to anything they perceive as unfair. If one child gets a piece of cake and another doesn't, the child who doesn't get the cake will be upset that she has been treated unfairly. This idea of fairness, connected in young children with very concrete experiences of comparing what they get with what someone else gets, develops into the abstract concept of justice as a child matures.

*In turn, our intellectual categories penetrate and affect our emotional categories.* For instance, if I were driving down a narrow street and a driver came right up behind my bumper and blew her horn, my first classification of her would likely be based on my experience of pushy people who demand to go first. My emotional reaction would likely be one of dislike. But if I knew that the person behind me was trying to get to the hospital where her husband was dying in the emergency room, my emotional reaction to her would be different because my intellect has reclassified her.

*We experience pleasure and enjoyment of the world around us with the intuitive intellect.* We catch sight of a flower and appreciate its beauty, not just its usefulness to us. We experience the flower as good whether or not we want to eat it. Human beings respond to the world in a way that the animals do not, with appreciation and curiosity. *It is our intuitive intellect that knows that something is good in itself,* that enjoys sunsets and autumn colors, history and poetry, art and music.

## Judging and Reasoning

There are many things that we don't immediately understand. Therefore we need the other functions of our intellect that make it possible for us to put things together. *The process of putting things together is what we call reason.* First, *judgment* decides whether or not there is a relationship between two things. I started thinking about a friend who lives far away and a few minutes later she called. Did I somehow sense that she was going to call? Was it a coincidence?

Then our intellect places these judgments into sequences, following the line of *reasoning* to see if something is true. X was seen near the scene of the crime. Did X have a motive? Did X have the means to commit the crime? Was someone else nearby? We do this all the time, both in science and in our everyday experience, both in our theoretical reasoning and in our practical reasoning.

Our intellect, theoretical and practical, intuitive and reasoning, allows us to experience the world in a way that is different from the way that animals do. The intellect knows the world in a much more complex way through language. When we see something we don't recognize, we ask ourselves, "What is that?" In other words, what kind of thing is it? What is it called? We do not just want to know whether we want to eat it or need to be afraid of it, although we do want to know these things. We want to know what it is. It is by means of language that we know this. It is through words, sentences, and stories that we can know the world that goes beyond the concrete world that animals know, that we can know the world of the spirit. *It is through language that we are able to develop the space between perception and action that allows us to make decisions, the particular kinds of choices that human beings make about good and bad, truth and falsehood.* But it is not the intellect that makes the decisions and choices. That is the job of another part of us.

# 7
# The Misunderstood Will

Our senses perceive the material world, but the senses never act alone. When human beings perceive something, the perception moves them to action. This movement is called an emotion. The intellect is the ability to perceive a reality that goes beyond the material world. When the intellect perceives something, it too is moved to action by that perception. This movement to action in the spiritual world is called the *will*. The will is the spiritual analog of the emotions. The fundamental emotions are love, desire, and pleasure. The fundamental actions of the will are love, desire, and joy. The fundamental action of the intellect is to see what is good and true. The fundamental action of the will is to love what is good and true.

## The Loving Will and the Executive Will

Just as the first step in our emotional life is love for what is good for us, *the foundation of the will is the loving will, the will that loves what is good not because it is useful to us, but simply because it is good.* This love reflects the love that God has for us. God did not create human beings to be his employees. He did not make Adam hoping that Adam would keep up the Garden of Eden for him at a reasonable price. God created us to enjoy his company, to be his friends.

This loving will is part of how we are made in the image and likeness of God. Like the animals, we can see that something is good for us and go after it in order to use it. Like God, we can see that something is good and beautiful and simply love it, whether or not it is useful to us. Just as in Genesis God rested on the seventh day and enjoyed what he had created, our loving will is characterized by a resting, passive enjoyment. When we see a beautiful sunset or hear beautiful music, we do not need to do anything except to love and enjoy it.

But God did not create the world as a still life. He created the world, and human beings, to move and grow and change. In Genesis, God created Adam and Eve so that they could develop according to their own human nature. God gave Adam and Eve dominion over the world. What did that mean? That God intended Adam and Eve to help all the other creatures develop according to their own natures. Paradise was a garden. What do gardeners do? They look at the condition of the soil and the climate and at the requirements of each kind of plant. Then they figure out how to help each plant to flourish. That is what God's dominion is about, and that is what human dominion is about. We are called to watch over the world that God has given us in such a way that every creature can grow and flourish according to its own nature.

In order to do this, we have to make decisions. *These decisions are the job of the executive will.* Each decision involves using the intellect to see what is really the case (the soil in our back yard is heavy red clay and it rains all the time) and also making a decision with the will according to the best interests of each being (I really like conifers, but conifers hate waterlogged soil, so I probably should not plant them in our backyard without amending the soil).

We are called on to make decisions about what is good for creatures, and the creature whose well-being we are most concerned about is ourselves. Our intellect is called on to see our real good. Since there are many conflicting goods, the intellect has quite a job to do. It is the task of the will to choose the greatest good for ourselves in any given situation. But choosing does not mean coercing ourselves. *The choices that the executive will makes grow out of the loving will. We choose what is good on the basis of love.*

People who say that we make our decisions based on pleasure and pain are correct in a limited way, but this limits pleasure and pain to the material world. If it feels good, do it. If it hurts, don't. The pleasures and pains of human beings are more complex than those of the animals.

## Loving Human Beings

One of the things that human beings enjoy most is the company of other human beings. This enjoyment goes beyond finding other people useful. We make this distinction all the time. "She didn't marry for love. She married for money." "He doesn't really love her. He just wants to use her." This love for other human beings, this approval and enjoyment of who they are simply in themselves, is a reflection and a revelation of God's love for us.

One of the primary actions of the loving will is to love other human beings. Each person is made in the image and likeness of God, no matter how badly that image has been battered. We are called on to love them in the way that God loves them—not because someone meets our own needs, or serves our own purposes, or does what we think is right. We are called to love other human beings in the overflowing way that a mother looks at her baby and sees the perfection that God has created. The people we are called on to love in this way are those least likely to call forth this love—the destitute, the battered, the bad. A Roman emperor commanded the deacon Lawrence to bring him the treasure that he thought the Christians had hidden away. Lawrence cheerfully agreed and showed up before the emperor the next day with a crowd of beggars and lepers.

We are also called upon to use the executive will in our interactions with other human beings. When we make decisions that affect others, we need to make our decisions as best we can on the basis of what would be truly good for others as well as what is good for ourselves. This is called loving our neighbors as ourselves.

The greatest action of the loving will is to love God. God is the greatest possible good, and he calls to us through each good thing that he has made in the world. *In loving good things, we learn to love God.* As we grow up and become able to perceive the good God who stands behind these good things, our love turns more and more to the giver of the gifts and less toward the gifts themselves. Since we are limited beings with limited time and attention, we have to choose what we care about most. As we are drawn more and more by the love of God, we are able to put aside goods that distract us from him, just as we would put aside other good activities to be with a person we love very much.

While our loving will desires to be with God, our executive will makes the choices that bring us closer to him. We are often drawn to goods that the loving will recognizes as good, but not as good as something else. We know we should choose one thing, but we are strongly drawn to another.

## Free Will and Habitual Will

Some ask whether our will is free since we can't always do what we wish we could do. We need to draw a distinction between our free will and our habitual will. God created each human being with a free will. We are not confined to the material world in our choices, nor are we bound by our instincts as the animals are. We are able to recognize a good greater than the immediate goods that surround us. When we recognize a greater good, we can follow it. At any moment, a human being has the ability to turn to what is good and true. This is our free will. Unfortunately, we do not have the ability to change all at once. Even when we are ashamed and sorry about what we have done, we find ourselves making the same choices. We do things the way we have always done them. This is our habitual will, and our habitual will is not quite so free.

Our habitual will is our default mode, and it operates in tandem with our Idealized Self. Unless we pay close attention to what we are doing, our habitual will takes over and makes the choices that we have always made. In fact, our habitual will makes choices before we are even aware of a choice to be made. While we are thinking about something else, it guides us to the place we have been many times before. Then our habitual will pushes us to make the choice we have made in the past, the choice that has brought us some pleasure or at least some relief from pain.

It may seem that we will never be able to choose differently, and we are often tempted to give up trying. How can we ever change? It can be helpful to think of the free will as the captain of a very large cargo ship. These ships are so large that it takes a long time to turn them around. The captain decides on his course and orders a sailor to turn the wheel—and nothing happens. Or nothing seems to happen. The sailor has to keep the wheel turned in the direction that the captain has ordered. The captain must take into account any approaching ships as well as the conditions of the ocean and the wind. He may have to make adjustments or take evasive action. But no matter what happens, the captain remains focused on his maneuver.

Similarly, it takes a long time to turn the habitual will so that it is heading where the free will wants to go. This is not easy. Our habits reflect the choices we have made in the past, and in the past these choices may have been what seemed best for us at the time, perhaps the only decision we thought we could make at the time. Life's circumstances have shaped our habits. We will fail as we try to change. But God knows our weaknesses. What he asks is that we remain focused on turning the ship of our habitual will. As difficult as this is, if we keep our hands on the wheel, God will help us. *We have to think in terms of small changes and little, even tiny, compromises.*

Chapters 11 through 17 contain techniques that Jim has used for many years in helping people to change. We will better succeed in changing when we use methods that enable the emotions, the intellect, and the will to work together. In the next chapter we will talk more about how the emotions, the intellect, and the will were created to work together. This will give us the basis for better using the techniques we present in Chapters 11 through 17.

# 8
# Putting It All Together

We have described our human abilities—the emotions, the intellect, and the will. But how do they fit together? We began our description of human nature by talking about the emotions of love, desire, and pleasure. *Our emotions are the power that moves us.* Whatever we do, whatever we learn, whatever we choose, our emotions are the source of our power to do it. If we try to ignore or get rid of our emotions because we fear they will move us in the wrong direction, we will either stand still or find ourselves riding a runaway emotion in the very direction we fear.

## The Rider and the Horse

The rider and the horse is a good image to explain the relationship between the intellect and will and the emotions. The rider—the intellect and the will—knows which direction he wants to go. The horse—the emotions—has the power to reach the destination. If the rider starves or beats the horse because he is afraid of the horse's power, the horse may waste away, leaving the rider with a much-diminished ability to get where he wants to go. Or the horse may rebel, taking off in any direction or even trying to throw the rider. If the rider loves the horse and cares for it, the horse will love the rider in turn. The horse will take the rider where he wants to go, taking pleasure in the relationship with the rider.

In an animal, the emotions act in the context of the kind of animal it is. Dogs behave in one way, cats in another. *In man, the emotions were created to act within the context of the intellect and the will.* Human beings do not feel right when their emotions are not integrated with the intellect and the will. After an animal eats what it desires, it doesn't say to itself, "Why did I do that? I really need to eat more vegetables and fewer sweets." The animal is moved by its instincts. When human beings are moved by their emotions to do something that the intellect does not see as good, they often feel regret.

The horse and the rider each have a particular kind of knowledge. Because our emotions are attuned to the physical world, they know a great deal about the material world that our intellect may not have noticed, and our emotions are constantly trying to tell the intellect what they know about the material world. We have many words for what our emotions are trying to tell us—a gut feeling, an intuition, a hunch, a funny feeling. *One of the intellect's important tasks is to listen to what the emotions are trying to tell it.* But we must also recognize that the intellect has the power to understand the world in a way that the emotions do not. *It is also important for the emotions to follow the guidance of the intellect and will.*

Imagine the horse and rider approaching a dark wood. Suddenly the horse shies and balks at going farther. The rider can react to this in different ways. He can beat the horse to make it go on. He can give the horse its head and let it run in the other direction. Or he can try to figure out why the horse balked. Is there a snake by the side of the road? Does the horse sense someone lying in wait behind a tree? Does the horse simply not like dark places? If the rider knows his horse, he will have some idea why the horse might be behaving this way. Once the rider understands the horse's reaction, he can decide what to do. If the horse loves and trusts the rider, the horse will go on even if it senses danger, because it knows that the rider has perceived its concerns and taken them into account in making a decision.

In the same way, when our emotions know that they are loved, cared for, and respected, they will follow the guidance of the intellect and the will. The emotions will push for what they see as good, but when they see that the intellect has determined that something else is better and the will has chosen this, *the emotions will eventually decide to use their power to support this decision. When the emotions habitually use their power to support the decisions that the intellect and will have made, the habitual will comes into line with the free will.* When this happens, we can do what we choose to do with the power and enjoyment that a rider feels when he and his horse are at one, galloping across a plain.

## Integrating the Emotions, the Will, and the Intellect

The process of integrating the emotions, the will, and the intellect is a long and difficult task. A child must begin by learning to love the good that exists in the material world. *If he does not experience love, desire, and pleasure in the material world, his experience of love, desire, and joy in the spiritual world will be profoundly damaged.* The greatest good in the material world that he can learn to understand is love, and he learns to understand what love is—kindness, tenderness, care—through his own experience of being loved. If a child does not experience love, he may know the concepts of kindness, tenderness, or care, but these concepts will not be integrated with his emotions. He may be able to give a dictionary definition of the words or to go through motions that he has observed, but he will not be able to experience what the words really mean. *A child who has not experienced human love will not be able to feel that God loves him.* He may well hold on to the *idea* that God loves him, but he will wonder what other people are experiencing when they speak of God's love.

As the child's intellect develops to maturity, so does his will. As he comes to understand the world in a deep and complex way, he is able to choose goods that are not readily apparent to the senses. He is able to share and do kind deeds. In other words, *he learns to love the world of the spirit in addition to the world of the senses, and out of this love he learns to choose the goods of the spirit when they are in conflict with the immediate goods of the senses.*

The root of this development is love. As a child grows up experiencing love and learning to love less obvious goods, he develops an appreciation of goods that are not simply material. His intellect is able to show him a wider range of goods—story-telling, art, music, science. These goods include the material world but go beyond it. *As his intellect perceives these goods, he learns to find pleasure in them.* His emotional life becomes refined and varied, and his understanding is enriched by the pleasure that these things give him. He learns to love ideas like mercy, justice, and truth.

The integration and cooperation of the pleasure emotions, the intuitive intellect, and the loving will are the foundation of our lives. We call these three parts of us working together the *heart.* This is what Scripture means when it tells us to love God with all our heart. As the pleasure emotions become integrated with the intuitive intellect and the loving will, and as they are guided and refined by them, they are called the *humane emotions.* The pleasures they seek are no longer only the pleasures of the senses, but also the pleasures of what it is that makes us human beings, the world of the spirit.

The greatest good is God. God is good beyond anything we can experience or imagine. We are called on to believe in God so that we can know him, and in knowing him love him with every fiber of our being, with our emotions, our intellect, and our will.

This friendship with God and with his other children is the purpose of our existence.

## The Role of the Pragmatic Emotions

Because we were created to live in the world, in time and space, as a mixture of dust and spirit, we were created to grow, change, and develop. We see a good and desire it, but we must do something to attain it. In the garden, Adam and Eve tended the plants as they grew. It is in this process of seeing things through, of bringing things to fruition, that the other parts of our human nature come into play.

*Our pragmatic emotions exist to serve the pleasure emotions.* They move us to do what needs to be done to get what we desire and to protect us from what would harm us. As we grow, these pragmatic emotions develop along with our practical intellect. It is the practical intellect's job to determine how to accomplish a particular good in a given situation. The executive will works with the practical intellect, choosing from among the practical intellect's options the best means to overcome an obstacle or to avert harm.

The pragmatic emotions play a critical role in this process. The emotions of hope and courage are the engines that keep the whole person moving when he faces an obstacle to what he desires. If a person feels only despair and fear, the intellect and will can still function, but they will be crippled. Depression is the feeling that it does not matter what we love or desire, since we cannot have what we love or desire anyway. When we feel this way, the intellect can suggest various solutions to a problem, but we cannot generate any interest in those solutions or choose among them because we cannot believe that any solution would really make any difference in how we feel.

*The intellect plays a critical role in the functioning of the prag-matic emotions.* The intellect can influence the emotions of fear and anger. I may be afraid of going to the doctor, but the intellect can influence the fear, calming it so I am willing to see her in order to obtain the good of being healed, even if the healing process involves discomfort. I may be angered by what someone says to me, but if I understand that the remark was not intended to hurt me, understanding can dissipate the anger.

Just as a child learns that not everything that he perceives as good is good for him, so he learns, under his parents' guidance, not to be overcome by fear and anger, but to let the intellect guide these emotions as they arise. A child learns that he may feel anger when another child grabs his toy, but that the anger needs to be guided into getting the toy back by some means other than by hitting. He learns that he may be afraid of going to the dentist, but he will feel much better in the long run if he goes. He learns that anger and fear are real and important, but that he must not make choices based on the emotions of anger and fear alone.

As a child develops, his pragmatic emotions become inte-grated with the practical intellect and the executive will. We call the integration of these three abilities the *mind.* When Scripture speaks of the mind, it refers to the integrated functioning of these abilities. The mind and the heart must in turn be integrated. When we integrate the mind and the heart, the mind must always serve the heart. *The pragmatic part of the soul must serve the part that loves.*

If the mind does not serve the heart, it begins to exalt itself. If the mind does not serve love, it finds its meaning in power and control. The heart sees the world, knows that it is good, and loves it. If the mind does not see the world through the eyes of love, it finds the world useful and tries to control it. A child who does not feel loved creates an Idealized Self. It is the mind that creates and sustains the Idealized Self. Even as the mind exalts itself, however, creating the grand and glorious Idealized Self, it still operates in the service of the heart. Whatever the Idealized Self may do, what it truly hopes to find is love.

## Beginning Our Renovation

Now we begin our renovation. Our intellect and our will are ready to help us carry out the task. They have two jobs: to be aware of the Idealized Self's defenses and to nurture the pleasure emotions. As we nurture the pleasure emotions, we will need the Idealized Self less and less. As we truly experience love, we can more easily let go of the tactics we have used to try to earn love. As we come to know what we love and what we desire, our pragmatic emotions can turn their energy toward helping us to get these things.

Before we begin, however, the authors would like to point out how the American emphasis on the pragmatic emotions contributes to many of the problems that concern us all.

# 9
# Overemphasizing the Pragmatic Emotions

American culture stresses the pragmatic emotions. After all, the most American of philosophies is called Pragmatism. We believe in what is useful, in getting things done. We emphasize getting ahead without stopping to ask ourselves what we need to get ahead of. We have little use for what we consistently refer to as the "frills" of art, music, philosophy, or poetry. People work hard to earn money to buy things. Children are encouraged from an early age to concentrate their efforts on what will make them successful. We judge people by how much they accomplish and how much money they make.

Researchers such as Dr. Stanley I. Greenspan, professor of clinical psychiatry, behavioral science, and pediatrics at the George Washington University Medical School, are sounding a warning note. In his book *The Growth of the Mind and the Endangered Origins of Intelligence,* Dr. Greenspan cites a growing body of research that points out the danger of overemphasizing what we call the pragmatic emotions at the expense of the pleasure emotions. Intelligence, he states clearly, grows out of and is dependent on emotional development. The core of emotional development is love. It is critical, Dr. Greenspan insists, that a child be loved simply for existing, not because she is cute or smart or can satisfy her parents' emotional needs. A child who is loved learns to love. Her pleasure emotions can mature into her humane emotions. When a child is not loved for who she is, the pleasure emotions will seek satisfaction in sensation, fun, thrills, and sensory stimulation. She develops destructive ways of both feeling and thinking.

With the American emphasis on the pragmatic emotions and the neglect of the pleasure emotions, we are creating a nation of Idealized Selves. People feel alone and unloved, cut off from others and from their real selves. In response to these feelings, people drive themselves to accomplish more, to earn more, to own more, all in the hope of experiencing the true satisfaction of being loved. At the same time, many people have lost any sense of who they are and what they desire. Since they are unable to feel their true desires, they try unsuccessfully to satisfy the pleasure emotions through working, shopping, and keeping busy.

Many children now prefer the virtual reality of television, computers, and video games to the real world around them. In these fantasy worlds, they find fantasy satisfactions that can quiet, just for a moment, the pain they feel because they do not feel loved just for who they are. This electronic stimulation can give no more than momentary satisfaction because it does not satisfy the real need to feel loved. We see children growing up glued to television sets and computers, trying to lose their pain in sex, drugs, and rock and roll, so desperate to satisfy their need to feel loved that they can think of little else.

American culture, Dr. Greenspan points out, is failing its children. Parents who feel overwhelmed by their children's needs place the children in daycare centers while they pursue the fulfillment of their own Idealized Selves. Workers in many of these centers, often poorly paid, undertrained, and overworked, have a very difficult time giving the babies and children in their charge any attention beyond the most basic physical care. If a daycare worker shows the ability to love children, she is often promoted to an administrative position where she has less contact with the children. The child who receives attention is often the child who cries the loudest. If a worker does form a loving bond with a child, the worker often moves on to another job, leaving the child devastated at the loss of love.

## How Schools Contribute to the Problem

As children suffer emotionally, their ability to perform intellectually falters. A child who is lonely and miserable cannot concentrate. A child who is desperate to please may learn to perform academic tasks, but she will experience learning as another hoop that she must jump through to please others, of no worth or interest in itself. A child who has learned that he can get attention by being demanding and aggressive will spend his time and energy disrupting the classroom. We have forgotten that before children can experience the love of learning, they must experience learning from those who love them.

In response to our children's problems in school, politicians demand that we return to "the basics." As school districts fall short of funds, they cut out "frills" like art and music. We have begun to emphasize testing students. Since teachers are rewarded on the basis of test scores, testing becomes the focus of school work and there is little time for anything except preparation for tests. Any sense that children might learn because they are interested in something or want to understand something is lost. Children have little time to explore their own interests or desires as teachers pile on homework in an attempt to meet test standards. Children experience school as being at war with their pleasure emotions. Our schools have become a major part of the problems they are trying to solve.

Parents, many of whom have never received the love they needed, try desperately to keep up with their jobs, their housework, their children. They hope that "quality time" spent with their children will make up for the fact that they see their children so seldom. And quality time is often time in which parents take their children to some activity or try to teach them something rather than time in which parents can simply enjoy their children's company. Parents run themselves ragged taking their children to lessons, games, and play dates. Everything is organized. Everything points to something useful.

The result is the overstimulation of the pragmatic emotions and the neglect of the pleasure emotions. Since the pleasure emotions receive no satisfaction, they remain the emotions of a small child. The pleasure emotions cannot mature and become integrated with the contemplative intellect and the loving will. They cannot mature into the humane emotions, and the pleasure that the humane emotions take in art, music, literature, and the company of others never develops. The pleasure emotions remain fixated on finding pleasure in sensory stimulation, thrills, fun, excitement, and in buying more things.

Even if children become involved in art or music, this often means practice instead of enjoyment, emphasizing lessons and professional development. Instead of a family singing together around the piano, we have children preparing for competitions. If the child doesn't show "promise" as a musician, music becomes something that someone else performs and the child experiences it only on CDs. The irony is how often the CDs contain music that protests against a culture that overemphasizes the pragmatic emotions and ignores the pleasure emotions.

Is it any wonder that life feels empty? Is it any wonder that children are full of despair? Is it any wonder that American children have such a high suicide rate?

# The Pragmatic Church

Christians also find themselves caught between a rock and a hard place. As churches struggle to carry out the injunction to feed the hungry and clothe the naked, they become busier and busier. Each new body that comes through the front door is seen as a recruit to carry the burden of doing good. Burnout is common. We create wholesome activities for our children, form committees to help the homeless, and spend our vacations building houses in Central America. We put the pleasure emotions on hold as we rush from project to project. We have lost all sense of finding joy simply in being with God. The authors recently saw a bumper sticker that said, "Jesus is coming. Look busy."

We tend to laugh at the physicians of the Colonial era who bled their patients, drawing blood from their veins no matter what disease the patient suffered from. It is clear to us that the cure these physicians used was itself dangerous. It is harder to see our own destructive attempts to solve the problems we face. Because the American devotion to pragmatism has produced material abundance, we tend to see pragmatism as the answer to all of our problems. But we are seeing another, darker side of that devotion to pragmatism in the problems our children are having today—school shootings, bullying, depression, and suicide. Like George Washington's physician, whose devotion to bleeding hurried the death of our first president, we can respond to our children's problems with the treatment we have always used. Or we can have the courage to question the way we have always done things and try another way.

# 10
# Trick and Treatment

Change means healing the emotional suffering that lies at the root of our conflicts. The Idealized Self can cease its vigilance only to the extent that the real self begins to develop, and the real self is full of pain. As we become aware of the pain, there will be many times when we want to give up. Keep in mind that *the time when we most want to give up is when we are closest to a breakthrough, closest to weakening some hold that the Idealized Self has on us*. The Idealized Self will put up a powerful fight. It will use every wile, every defense at its disposal. It will fight most desperately when it knows that it is about to lose a battle. The Idealized Self will tell you that you cannot bear the pain, that you cannot change, that the whole process is a lie, that it has a really good new Idealized Self ready to take over, and that this Idealized Self will really work this time. You will discover that you really want to move to a new house, buy a car, serve the poor in Ethiopia, serve on the building committee, or become a novelist. Anything except the painful, daily slogging of dealing with these feelings.

It is just at these painful points that hope and courage can come to the rescue of the real self instead of defending the Idealized Self. Each time we stick to it, each time we refuse to escape from the pain of the real self into the false promises of the Idealized Self, we bring our emotions of hope and courage more firmly into the service of the real self. As the real self becomes stronger, we can begin to abandon the defenses that the Idealized Self has built.

We need humility if we are going to change. Not the false humility of the Idealized Self that whispers how awful we are and that we can never change. True humility recognizes that we are dependent on God, that we cannot imagine the real self that God created us to be. Humility accepts that what we value most in ourselves may be the very thing that God wants to change. If we are to nurture our real self, we must allow God to show us that self step by step. Our real self is a gift from God. People talk about finding themselves, as if the self were a misplaced set of keys. Humility recognizes that we cannot find a self. We must be willing to receive a self.

## Seeking the Real Self

To allow our real self to develop, we have to pay attention to it. How can we do this? *Two of the most important times of the day are first thing in the morning and just before we go to bed, two traditional times of prayer. At these two times we need to turn to God, first to prepare for the day and then to review the day to see how our healing has gone.*

First thing in the morning and last thing at night sit down and turn your attention to God. God often uses two ways to let us know what he wishes to heal at a given point in our journey. The first is in our reading. While God can speak to us in anything we read, it is important to begin the day with some spiritual reading. If you are from the Christian tradition, it is good to read the Bible. There are many courses of Bible readings. Choose one. Whatever spiritual reading you choose, listen to what God is saying to you. Read it once. Then read it again and see what leaps out at you—a word, a phrase, an idea. Hold that word or phrase in your mind. Ask yourself, if I knew what God wanted me to work on today, what would it be? Wait quietly and see what bubbles up. For the rest of the day keep that thought in mind and see how it applies to the day's events. At night just before you go to bed, sit with God and listen to what comes into your mind from the depths of your being.

*The Idealized Self will do anything to prevent you from doing this.* You will oversleep in the morning. Just before bedtime you will be strangely attracted to television. You will be too tired or too busy. You will find this time irritating and boring. The Idealized Self is convinced that it has the only solution to your pain, and it takes that job very seriously. The Idealized Self believes that any suggestion of real change is a trick, and it will try to trick you into abandoning the effort to change because it wants to protect you from more pain.

Our first impulse when this happens is often to be impatient and irritated with the Idealized Self. Remember that the Idealized Self developed to deal with the impatience and irritation that others felt toward the real self. When the Idealized Self perceives any irritation, it redoubles its effort to protect itself. *One of the most important steps we can take in our healing is to allow ourselves to feel compassion for ourselves.* If you saw a small child standing by the side of the road, alone, hungry, and afraid, would you say to yourself, "Look at that stupid child. Why doesn't he find something to eat and clean himself up?" More likely you would be moved with compassion for the child.

In the same way, you can feel compassion for the lonely, frightened, suffering part of yourself and for the hopeful, courageous Idealized Self that tries to protect you. When the Idealized Self trips you up, when you oversleep and feel that you have no time to sit with God, instead of berating yourself, thank your Idealized Self for protecting you. Put your arm around your Idealized Self and give it a hug. Then sit with God, if only for a minute.

God also speaks to us about what needs to be healed through what happens to us during the day. We tend to see things as *happening* to us. The word *happen,* like the word *happy,* comes from a root referring to what comes about by chance. Instead of seeing what happens to us as things that occur by chance, we can see them as opportunities that God gives us for change. We can respond to each difficult situation as an opportunity to watch our own emotions and see what the Idealized Self is up to. Then before we go to bed we can look at those emotions and allow God to help us with them. This attitude can give us hope. Our lives are not a random concatenation of events. As we use what happens to us each day as an opportunity to change, *we will begin to feel better.*

## Seeking Understanding

These days when someone receives a medical diagnosis, he often goes directly to the library or to the Internet to gather as much information as he can about the illness. We also need to do this for our emotional healing. We need to use our intellect to learn as much as we can about how the Idealized Self works. Then we can gently tell the Idealized Self that while we appreciate all that it has done for us, it doesn't need to do this any more.

In Chapter 24, we give a list of books that many people have found helpful in emotional healing. These books are in print and are often available at the local public library. Get these books. *Read them. Read them again. And again.* You will not understand everything the first time you read them, but you will understand more each time you reread them. You will be able to understand these books better if you read and reread this book along with them.

*Be ready for the voice that tells you that this is all useless or hopeless, that you can never change, that you are trapped forever.* These feelings are the Idealized Self and its defenses, ready to protect you from yet another hurt or disappointment. Do not argue with the Idealized Self. The Idealized Self is doing what it has done to keep you alive all your life. Listen to the voice, but don't believe what it tells you. *Instead, listen to the feelings behind the voice—the fear, the despair, the rage—and hear what they have to tell you about the experiences that caused these feelings in the first place.*

Healing is a journey that takes time. God does sometimes heal people suddenly, but most often healing is gradual, not because God is testing us or being mean, but because we have to get used to being healthy. If God suddenly healed us emotionally, we wouldn't know who we were or how to act, and the people around us wouldn't know how to react to us either. So in the same way that we usually recover slowly from a physical illness, *we are healed emotionally one step at a time.*

*Don't be surprised if other people don't respond positively to what you are doing.* When people don't know what to expect, fear begins to whisper all kinds of terrible things—that the person who is changing will suddenly run off to Mexico, quit his job to try a career in acting, or demand that everything be done differently. You need to respect other people's fear. If someone seems open to an explanation of what you are doing, share it with him. If not, pray about what to do. God does not call people to healing only to have them crushed back into suffering forever.

Most of all, know that God truly loves you and wants to heal you. This can seem very unreal in the midst of growing and changing, when you are feeling the pain that you have not been strong enough to feel before. But God always goes before you as you take each step. He will send a person, a book, *whatever you need for the next step of your journey.* You are never alone, you are never abandoned. God knows each of us in the depths of our hearts and comes to us exactly where we are. Be still, and God will speak to you and lead you.

Remember to read this chapter over and over again, because you will not be able to absorb all the suggestions the first time you read it, or even the second time.

# PART II

# How to Do It

# 11
# Listening to Your Emotions

In the old television show *Lassie,* a brave collie usually showed up at her master Timmy's house barking loudly. Timmy's mother turned to watch Lassie. "What is it, girl? What are you trying to tell me?" Of course, Lassie was trying to tell her that Timmy was in danger and that someone needed to follow Lassie to the place where Timmy needed to be rescued. If no one would listen to her, Lassie would bark louder and jump around, perhaps even grabbing someone's clothing in her teeth. Anything to get people's attention and lead them to Timmy. We tend to think of our painful emotions as bad, as something we need to get rid of. It is more useful to think of our painful emotions as being like Lassie. The emotions know that there is a problem, but they can't use words to tell anyone what the problem is. The emotions can only bark and nip to get our attention and lead the way to the trouble.

Our painful emotions will lead us to where the trouble lies if we will just follow them. *We are used to seeing our emotions as caused by something outside ourselves.* We think that we are full of rage because someone has mistreated us. We are sure that our feelings are hurt because someone has said something unkind to us. When we assume that something outside ourselves is responsible for how we feel, we tend to believe that we have only two choices in responding to our emotions: to act on them or to push them aside. There is a third alternative. *We can listen to our emotions.* Our emotions have a lot to tell us, not only about the world around us, but also about ourselves.

77

## Habits of Responding to the World

Out of millions of tiny everyday childhood experiences within our family, each of us began to interpret the world around us in ways that we weren't even aware of. We expected people to behave in certain ways, and we knew what that behavior meant. We responded to our experiences with the emotions that seemed to protect us most effectively at the time. Did we respond to feeling hurt by becoming angry? By feeling fear and withdrawing? By trying to please people in the hope of earning their love? Over time, these emotional responses shaped our whole personalities.

Each of us has many habitual ways, large and small, of responding emotionally to the world, and these emotional habits served us well as we were growing up. But often as we move outside the orbit of our families, we find that these habitual responses don't work any more. For instance, if a child's parents have tried to control his emotions and actions, the child may find that the only way he can assert himself is to behave passive-aggressively. This means that while he is afraid to show his aggression and resistance to his parents, he does express his aggression in passive ways that defeat his parents without confronting them openly. He forgets to do what they ask him to do or he does it wrong. He loses things. He may feel that this is the only way he can deal with his parents' demands on him. But he is also likely to behave passive-aggressively in school, forgetting his homework, being late to school, or not hearing what his teacher says to him. When the child behaves this way, he sees himself as defeating people who are making demands on him and trying to control him. Unfortunately, the child defeats himself with his passive-aggressive behavior by doing poorly in school.

*The emotional responses we develop in our families are so deeply embedded in us that we tend to see our problems as caused by the world around us.* We don't get the respect we deserve. Our spouses don't love us. Our bosses are too demanding. *We tend not to realize that our own behavior and emotional habits call forth responses from other people that reinforce the way we see the world.*

The child who behaves passive-aggressively in school often brings out feelings of impatience in his teacher, and his teacher may try to find ways to get the child to remember his homework or get to school on time. The child recognizes the teacher's feelings of impatience as similar to his parents' feelings when he resists their attempts to control him, and he feels right at home with the teacher's response. He perceives any attempt to get him to school on time as an attempt to control him, not as an attempt to help him. *In the child's mind,* the situation becomes a struggle for control. The child is likely to feel hostile toward his teacher and to resist her efforts to help him. As a child like this grows up, he is likely to develop an Idealized Self that sees itself as a Clint Eastwood figure, fighting alone against powerful forces trying to control and destroy him. No matter how much harm such a person does to himself by his own passive-aggressive behavior, no matter how much hostility he arouses in others by his own hostile behavior, he sees outside forces as causing his problems.

## How to Go About Changing

If we are going to change, we need to examine our emotions and let them tell us about our Idealized Self and its habits. We need to listen *when we find ourselves either trying not to feel an emotion or flooded by an emotion.* For instance, a person may find herself irritated by something her husband has said, done, or forgotten to do. Some try to ignore the irritation. Others voice the irritation vigorously, bringing up several other examples of the same irritating behavior.

The third alternative is to *withdraw from the situation and listen to the irritation.* This does not mean feeling how irritating your spouse is. You need to think about why you are so irritated, not about why your spouse is so irritating.

Sit down alone and listen to the voice of the irritation. Ask God for help. Then let the feeling run free inside you. As the emotion runs free, do nothing except to listen to it. As you listen, ask yourself *exactly what* about your spouse's behavior bothers you.

It is very helpful to give the emotion its real name. Its real name may surprise you. What you have called "irritation" might more accurately be called "rage." We tend to downplay emotions that the Idealized Self wants to deny, calling them by a name that denies the strength of the emotion. It is edifying to call an emotion by its correct name. Say to yourself, "I'm feeling hostile." Or bitter. Or resentful. Do not condemn yourself for any emotion that you feel. It is there for a reason. Just watch it and notice what it does. Don't act it out. Don't punch someone because you feel hostile.

If you listen very carefully to the emotion, you may find another emotion mixed in with it. For instance, when a woman feels rage at seeing her husband flirt with another woman, she may hear beneath the rage the voice of fear that her husband does not find her attractive. She may feel jealous. If a woman feels flooded with fear when she sees her husband flirting, under the fear she may hear rage that her husband would humiliate her in this way or desert her emotionally.

Whatever emotion you find yourself feeling, *do not try to change the way you feel.* If you decide not to feel rage or fear, you will simply stuff the rage or fear out of sight to fester. Do not act out the feeling. Notice how you are feeling and watch the emotion at work. Do certain things regularly arouse this feeling in you? Ask yourself, "When was the first time that I remember feeling this emotion?"

Let the emotion talk to you. Let the emotion tell you what has hurt you, what you have been afraid of. Imagine yourself holding the emotion in your hands. Touch it. Feel it. You are likely to find images coming into your mind. No matter how strange the image, hold it in your mind and allow it to speak. The image may be visual, it may be a sound or a smell. Let the image grow. Feel all the feelings that the image brings with it. Very likely a situation or event from your childhood will come into your mind. Feel all the feelings that the memory of that event brings with it.

An example may make this clear. A woman had been quarreling with her husband. As usual, he ended the quarrel by walking away. The woman found herself flooded with rage as her husband stomped out the back door and slammed the door behind him. Instead of raging at her husband for his bad behavior, she went up to her bed, lay down, and began to listen to the rage. Flood after flood of rage washed over her. Then she tried to figure out exactly what had bothered her. Suddenly she realized that her rage had peaked when she heard the click of the back door as her husband walked away.

As she let the click of the door echo through her feelings, she was flooded with fear. She let the fear grow, even though the fear was so strong that she almost threw up. An image came to her— the image of a very tiny child in her crib. Again she let the image grow and felt the emotions that the child in the crib was feeling. She saw her mother, her face dark with rage, standing over her. "If you can't behave," her mother said to her, "I'll just leave you here until you learn how to behave." Her mother turned and walked out of the room, slamming the door behind her.

Rage, fear, and despair flooded through her. She knew that her mother would leave her alone in her room for many hours, alone, hungry, thirsty, afraid. She remembered all the times her mother had left her alone and helpless. Now, each time this woman heard the door slam shut behind her husband, she felt the same rage, fear, and despair that she had felt when her mother walked away and left her helpless. She experienced her husband's behavior as the cause of her rage, fear, and despair.

Her husband's behavior was the *occasion* of her rage. Walking away was not the best way to deal with the situation. But her husband's behavior was *not the cause* of her rage. Her feelings were far out of proportion to her husband's behavior, and these feelings got in the way of really discussing with her husband what had caused the quarrel in the first place. The woman began to listen to what her emotions were really telling her, that she had felt rage, fear, and despair when her mother had walked away from her, pulling the door closed behind her and leaving her alone. She was finally able to feel compassion for herself and to cry for all that she had suffered.

Then she was able to recognize that she was no longer tiny, no longer helpless in her crib. She was able to tell her husband about what had happened to her. She told him that she realized that her rage was excessive and that she wanted to change. After she explained her feelings to her husband, he listened to his feelings and realized that his mother had been a hostile and bitter woman, forcing him to listen to her tirades each day until he escaped by running out of the house.

When the woman listened to her emotions, they led her to the experience of being repeatedly abandoned by her mother. She recognized her own suffering and felt compassion for herself. Then she and her husband were able to help each other overcome their infantile fears.

## Listening to Your Impulses

Most of us have something we use to avoid feeling painful emotions—alcohol, drugs, cigarettes, food, caffeine, sex, television, shopping, work. If you listen to your emotions, you will realize that right before you feel the impulse to go shopping, to have a drink, or to eat a candy bar, you usually feel what seems like unbearable pain. Just for a moment, do not follow the impulse to do whatever you do to avoid your painful emotions. Do not take a drink. Do not eat. Do not light a cigarette. Do not turn on the television. Just for a moment.

Don't tell yourself that you will never again take a drink or eat chocolate. That is the Idealized Self trying to trip you up. Ask God for help. Then ask yourself what happened that made you feel so bad. It could be something that someone said to you. It could be a feeling of failure or a feeling of inadequacy or help-lessness. It could be something as simple as a particular time of day, such as dinnertime, that was usually painful when you were a child. Sit down and listen to the feelings. This does not neces-sarily mean that you will never again have a drink or go shop-ping. Painful emotions often speak a little bit at a time. But each time you listen to the emotions instead of trying to banish them with drugs, alcohol, or food, you will rescue a little bit more of yourself from the suffering that you have endured.

We rescue ourselves from the experiences that have caused us suffering by bringing these experiences into the light of the intellect. When young children are hurt or traumatized, they experience the suffering with the emotions and the understand-ing of a small child. Because the emotions are so painful, the Idealized Self *encapsulates* these feelings, pushing them out of awareness. When we push the emotions out of awareness, we also isolate them from the process of growing up. As we grow up, we can learn to understand what happens to us in a more grown-up way. We learn that others may hurt us not because we are bad, but because they have themselves been hurt. We learn to defend ourselves in ways that small children cannot do, using words to solve disagreements or to object to the bad behavior of others.

Encapsulated emotions are not influenced by what we learn as we grow up. They are trapped at the level of development at which they occurred. Many of these emotions are preverbal, emotions that we felt before we were able to talk. Because they are still the emotions of a young child, they move us to act as a small child would act. When we finally bring these emotions into the light of the intellect, we give these emotions words to speak, to tell us what happened and why we feel the way we feel. Let us make very clear here that when we talk about bringing these emotions into the light of the intellect, we are *not* in any way talking about "explaining the emotions away." In fact, we are talking about just the opposite of explaining the emotions away. We can free ourselves from our suffering only when we clearly see the suffering that we have undergone and recognize how painful it was. When we bring these emotions into the light of the intellect, we give these emotions the recognition and affirmation that they have never had. We are finally showing ourselves compassion.

## The Importance of Talking

Talking about your emotions is the primary way of bringing your emotions into the light of the intellect. This does not mean discussing what happened to you in an abstract way. You need to allow yourself to actually experience the fullness of the emotions. This often involves *action* such as crying, yelling at the imagined presence of the person who hurt you, or hitting pillows. You need to let yourself go back to your experiences and react to them as you were not allowed to react to them when you were small. As you experience the emotions, large muscle exercise such as walking, running, or working out can help dispel the physical intensity of the emotions. But as you let yourself experience the emotions, you also need to help the emotions to use words to express themselves.

You need to share these experiences with someone who can give you support, understanding, and compassion. Often family members are *not* the best people to talk to unless they are working on their own emotions. Family members in the grip of their own Idealized Self may simply be distressed by any attempt to bring up emotions that they are working hard to deny.

Friends can be very supportive. You have to be careful, however, that the friend you talk to about your emotions does not get caught up in your emotions because he or she has experienced similar suffering. A person caught up in your feelings does not simply offer empathy and understanding, but rather takes on your feelings. For example, a person may become enraged at what happened to you, echoing and encouraging your rage. If a friend seems to be encouraging you to act out the emotions before you have fully experienced the emotions and thrown the light of the intellect on them, be cautious about sharing your emotions. This is particularly important if the friend is encouraging you to confront someone, especially a family member. Some people act out their own hostility by encouraging others to engage in confrontation. While they are not willing to admit their own desire to confront people, they enjoy seeing others engage in conflict.

Psychotherapists, counselors, and support groups can be very helpful. Psychotherapists and counselors are trained to help you to understand your emotions. It can be wonderful to talk to those in a support group who have suffered the same things that you have. They usually will not tell you that it wasn't that bad or that you should snap out of it.

Writing is another good way to let your emotions speak. Don't worry if you can't spell correctly or your grammar is shaky. This writing is for your edification. If the first sixty sentences consist of "I can't stand it," that's fine. Just keep writing. Put on paper what happened to you and how you felt, what you wanted to tell people but couldn't, what you wanted to do. Then put the writing aside. When you read it again at some later point, you may notice things in what you've written that you hadn't noticed before. This can lead you to a new understanding about your experiences.

## The Idealized Self and Feeling Better

As you bring your emotions out of the darkness of their suffering and into the light of the intellect, the power of these emotions will begin to diminish. You will begin to feel better. *It is very important that you notice that you are feeling better.* The Idealized Self will not want you to notice how much better you are feeling. The Idealized Self will tell you that it may be better now, but it's only temporary. The Idealized Self will insist that soon everything will be back to normal. The Idealized Self is a set of emotional habits, and habits are hard to break. Our old emotional habits served us well as children, and it can be frightening to give them up. How will we know who we are, if we aren't who we were?

*Very soon after you have experienced an emotional healing, the Idealized Self will sneak up on you.* It will tell you that something you said or did was incredibly stupid. It will laugh at you. It will tell you that other people were laughing at you, that you made a fool of yourself. These attacks by the Idealized Self can be extremely painful. The Idealized Self is fighting for its life. When you find yourself starting to feel awful about something you have said or done, talk to someone about it right away. You will be tempted to try to deal with it yourself to avoid humiliating yourself further by letting anyone know how stupid you are. Perhaps the best escape from an attack by the Idealized Self is to talk to someone who can help you to see what is happening.

# 12
# Attention, Media, and the Idealized Self

The first step in listening to our emotions is to take back our attention. Attention is the first action of love. Attention does not just happen. We *give* our attention, and *our attention is the most valuable thing we have to give.* When a child wants love, what does she try to get first? Her mother's attention. How can someone hurt our feelings? Fail to pay attention to us. *What part of ourselves is choosing what we pay attention to?* Is it our real self? Or is it our Idealized Self?

The Idealized Self has an enormously powerful ally—the media—that keeps us from paying attention to our real self. Think about how many hours of your life you give to television, radio, magazines, newspapers, sports programs, video games, cell phones, and the Internet. Then imagine what your life would be like without these media. Try an experiment. The next time you want to pay attention to any medium, pay attention instead to what you are feeling. At first you will probably feel irritation and boredom. *The Idealized Self uses irritation and boredom to mask our deeper emotions.* Sit with the irritation and boredom as long as you can and listen to what your emotions are telling you. Ask yourself what happened to you and what you were feeling just before you felt the impulse to turn on the television or pick up a magazine.

The media support the Idealized Self by presenting imaginary grand, glorious, and quick solutions to real problems, solutions cloaked in compelling scenarios. We feel *temporary* relief from our pain as we watch someone else solve problems easily. We are drawn to the media because of this temporary relief. Unfortunately, *the imaginary solutions to problems do nothing to touch the real pain that our real self feels.* The media are a narcotic that we use to dull our pain. If someone experienced chest pains, you would not give him pain medication. You would take him to the doctor to find out what was really happening. Similarly, we need to address the real pain that the real self is feeling.

We are not suggesting that you simply give up all media right now. The Idealized Self loves to present us with this kind of all-or-nothing solution. We are suggesting that as you watch television, listen to the radio, and read magazines, you might think about how they encourage you to identify with the Idealized Selves they present and how this strengthens your own Idealized Self. If you use them effectively, the media can be an excellent clue to the workings of your own Idealized Self.

## Your Idealized Self and the Media

As you watch television or listen to the radio, notice the emotions that the people on the program are feeling. Are they hostile? Are they resentful? Are they full of indignation? Are they loving? Listen to the tone of their voices. Watch the expressions on their faces. Ask yourself what you are feeling as you watch them. Think of the various forms that the Idealized Self takes. Are these people self-affirming? Self-denying? Paralyzed? What part of the Idealized Self do these people identify with? With a great mission? With their own high standards? With their great accomplishments? Do they see other people as the source of all their problems? Do they make fun of others? Do they present other people as evil, stupid, or incompetent? The *content* of the program is not important. There are shows for all interests, all beliefs, all political viewpoints. Ask yourself, is there an Idealized Self at work here? If so, what emotions in you resonate with this Idealized Self? When you watch this program, do you feel hostile? Indignant? Resentful? Powerful?

When you watch a drama, what situations in the plot arrest your attention? Do you enjoy watching programs about love relationships? About people in danger from criminals? About people threatened by powerful interests? About people threatened by unknown dangers? About people surrounded by incompetent idiots? What do you feel as you watch sports programs? Whom do you laugh at when you watch comedy programs? How do you feel when you watch violence on television or in a movie? Does watching violence allow you a release for your own feelings of rage and hostility?

Ask yourself another question. Do you feel closer to the people you are watching or listening to than you do to the people who surround you in everyday life? What emotions do you share with these media characters that you do not share with your spouse, your children, your friends? What programs do you most enjoy discussing with others?

As you begin to pay attention to the media's reflections of your Idealized Self, do not try to change. Simply observe what is happening. When you decide to change something all at once, the Idealized Self generally steps in to take over the process, diverting you with another grand and glorious plan to overcome the real self. Just pay attention to what your Idealized Self is doing. Does your Idealized Self want you to see yourself as moral and upright? As kind and loving? As hardworking and responsible? As powerful and in charge? As part of a great cause? There is nothing wrong with any of these things in themselves. But ask yourself how you feel about those you see as immoral. As unloving. As lazy and irresponsible. As dependent and weak. As opposed to your cause.

If you find yourself full of rage, it is helpful to ask if you could be feeling hostile toward those who don't return your love. Could you be fascinated by what you find immoral? Could you be feeling that you have been responsible at an enormous cost to yourself? Could you be feeling weak and vulnerable? Could you long to be part of a great cause so that you do not feel alone?

## Listening to Your Real Self

As you ask yourself these questions, listen for the voice of emotions that you have tried to ignore. These emotions may not be clear, or logical, or pleasant. You may have read stories about children who were locked in a closet for years. When they were rescued, these children needed special care and time to develop. It is helpful to think of your real self as a child who was locked in a closet. Your real emotions expect to be ignored and abused. They do not expect to be heard.

We are not telling you to act on these emotions. Quite the opposite. We are not suggesting that you blast people with hostile diatribes, decide that you're tired of being responsible and run off to the Caribbean, or run out to a singles bar. When you listen to your emotions at this stage of development, *it is very, very difficult to understand exactly what they are saying.* What they are trying to convey to you may not be what they seem to be saying. There is a great temptation to switch from one kind of Idealized Self to another—to change from being a doormat to telling everyone off, to change from being a pillar of the church to being a swinging single. Doing this will short-circuit your growth and change. Simply listen to your emotions.

Once you begin to listen to the emotions that you have not wanted to experience, those emotions will begin to tell you what they need. If you are going to nurture these emotions and give them what they really need, you have to nurture them in the right way. The media are full of ideas for nurturing yourself, for indulging yourself, for rewarding yourself. Notice that most of these ideas involve *buying* something—clothes, cars, electronics, body products, expensive chocolate, exotic vacations.

Most of the media's ideas for nurturing yourself involve *acting out.* That is, they are suggesting that you *act on the emotions without really understanding what the emotions are trying to tell you.* There is nothing wrong with buying bubble bath, chocolate, or a new car. But if you buy the item without taking the time to let your emotions tell you what they *really* need, *the emotions will not be satisfied.* They will be quieted for a moment, but soon the same emotions will begin to nip at you again because you have given them something that television has suggested that they *should* want instead of what they really want.

The noise of the media stands in the way of knowing what your emotions really need and want. The media play on the fact that many people are unhappy and full of pain. Television and magazines are full of tips for feeling better and suggestions for stuff to buy in order to quiet the pain. But the stuff that the media try to sell you will not quiet the pain. In fact, the stuff will only increase the pain, because once you own it, you tend to feel not only the original pain, but also the burden of taking care of the stuff and disappointment that owning the stuff has not made you feel better. However, it isn't helpful to decide that you are not going to buy any more stuff when you feel bad. This is the voice of the Idealized Self. Growth comes through little changes and small compromises.

The important thing is to listen to your emotions. Pay attention to what the Idealized Self is doing, but do not try to fight it. Two books by Karen Horney are very helpful in understanding the workings of the Idealized Self. The first book is *Our Inner Conflicts.* The second book is *Neurosis and Human Growth.* Both of these books give excellent descriptions of the various forms of the Idealized Self and how all Idealized Selves work. As you notice the emotions that your Idealized Self wants you to ignore, you can begin to nurture your real self. As your real self grows, you will be able to let go of the defenses that the Idealized Self uses.

# 13
# Nurturing Your Pleasure Emotions

The first step in nurturing your pleasure emotions is to *stop*. Stop trying to earn love by taking care of everyone or trying to be good. Stop trying to earn love by accomplishing things. Stop trying to earn love by being right. This first step is difficult, because the Idealized Self will tell you that you aren't doing these things to earn love, you are doing them because you want to. Each time you feel moved to serve on still another committee or to accomplish something outstanding, ask yourself what would happen if you did not do this. Then ask yourself what you hope will happen if you do.

It's likely you're afraid that either God or the people around you will be annoyed with you if you do not serve on the committee. In other words, you are afraid of losing love. It's likely you hope that people will admire you if you accomplish something. In other words, you are hoping to earn love.

*As long as you try to earn love, you will never feel loved.* You will not be able to feel love for the people around you because you will be busy trying to earn their love. Imagine that you could really experience deep feelings of love for those around you. Imagine that you could experience the love and presence of God. Imagine that you could feel loved, not because you've reached some ideal of perfection, but just for who you are. Visualize yourself being loved. If you can't see yourself being loved, you are not likely to feel loved.

Everything in our lives begins in love and flows out of love. A baby's earliest experiences are of her mother's love and care. That love and care are very concrete—milk, warmth, being held and rocked. If our need for love and nurture is met, our emotions grow and develop. But if we have been deprived or abused, this development is interrupted. If we do not experience love as infants, our infantile need for love does not mature. The neediness remains, as urgent and as simple as the neediness of a young child. No matter how intellectually sophisticated we may become as we grow up, our need for love remains stuck at the age at which we did not feel loved. That is why, when we begin to change, we must go back to the stage of life in which we felt deprived.

Because our needs are those of a young child, *what we think we want is often not what our emotions try to tell us that they really need.* For example, if you were deprived of the emotional warmth and closeness that a tiny child needs when her mother feeds her, you may feel driven to eat in an attempt to fill the need for warmth and closeness. You may eat too much not because you feel hunger for food, but rather because you feel hunger for warmth and closeness. The foods that you are most likely to crave are foods with the simple and strong tastes that children crave— sweets, fats, carbohydrates, comfort foods.

In the face of this, you may despise yourself, wondering why you can't control yourself. But if you listen to your feelings and notice what you are really craving, you can begin to give yourself what you genuinely need. You can feel the real longing for your mother's love, and you can give yourself care and com- passion. You can use the resources that you have as an adult to create the conditions in which your stunted emotions can grow up, guiding your emotions in their growth and integrating your infantile feelings with your adult self. You can also ask for help from others.

# Learning to Experience Goodness

*Allow yourself to experience goodness.* To feel goodness is to learn to love. Because you need to allow your emotions to begin developing at the point in your life at which you did not feel loved and cared for, you will probably need to begin by experiencing goodness simply with your senses. You need to allow your senses to love and desire what seems good to them. To do this *you need to pay attention to exactly what it is that you desire.* If you felt unloved as a small child, what you desire is usually very concrete—to suck on something, to be stroked, to be held. Listen to the desire, just as you listen to your emotions when you feel bad. Pinpoint exactly what you want. Do you want to suck on something? Some people suck on a piece of hard candy or, if they can do it in private, even a pacifier or their thumb. *Pay attention to the satisfaction* that comes from sucking. Don't do anything else while you experience that satisfaction.

If you long to be held and stroked, go to a massage therapist. Going to a massage therapist may be one of the best things that you can do for yourself. Many of us were not held and cuddled when we were small. We crave being stroked and touched. Massage is one of the safest and most satisfying ways to experience this. Find a massage therapist you are comfortable with. As you are massaged, really pay attention to each stroke. You may find other emotions arising. For instance, you may find yourself afraid that the table is going to collapse. Pay attention to the fear and let it tell you about the times when you were afraid that someone was going to "let you down." Then return your attention to the satisfaction of being touched. *Allow yourself to really experience the satisfaction.* If you cannot go to a massage therapist, or between your visits, stroke your own arms. Rub your own feet or the back of your neck. Most people burst into tears when they first experience the joy of infantile pleasures. This is a sign of healing.

If you find yourself craving the strong tastes that children love—fats, sweets, carbohydrates—give yourself what you crave, but in a measured way. Give yourself one piece of chocolate and *pay attention* to the taste of the chocolate rather than gulping down a whole bag of candy that you don't even allow yourself to taste.

# Reclaiming Our Senses

The modern world overstimulates our senses. We have learned to cope with sensations bombarding us at an enormous rate. Television and movies accustom us to instantaneous shifts in what we see and hear. As a result, we are so busy simply coping with the constant stream of sense stimulation that our senses have no autonomy. We are invaded and overwhelmed by our surroundings without even being aware of it.

*Minimize outside stimulation.* Turn off the television. Turn off the radio. Turn off the music. At first you will feel lost. The old joke says that one day the wind stopped blowing in North Dakota and everyone fell over. When the overstimulation stops, all the energy we have put into dealing with it is not quite sure what to do with itself.

It takes time to reclaim your senses. Sit quietly. Don't try to notice anything. Don't try to feel anything. As you sit, make yourself comfortable and see what you notice. Don't actively direct your attention. See what catches your eye, or your ear, or your nose. You have five senses. They all need to grow. *At this point you are likely to remember something extremely important that you must do at this very instant.* The Idealized Self does not want to let go. Put what you have to do aside and let your mind and your senses wander.

If you can only feel a sort of jittery feeling, then that's what you feel. Listen to it. Experience your scalp, your eyes, your lips. What are your hands doing? Stick with the process of experiencing your own senses. You are reclaiming them for your own. If you were going to start running after years of sitting, you would start out with little jogs, slowly increasing the length and speed of your running. The same holds true for your senses. Take time throughout the day for brief moments of sensing. Enjoy the smells and sights on the street or in your home. Be aware of anything that offends you. That is important, too.

Whenever possible, *do one thing at a time.* Do not multitask. If you are eating, really eat. Smell the food. Taste the food. Notice the aftertaste. Do you like it? What would you like to eat? This process is very important. Eating is central to our lives, and a myriad of feelings surround it. Is one of them enjoyment? Don't read while you eat. Don't listen to music while you eat. Especially do not work while you eat. If you find that you can't really enjoy eating, listen to your emotions and let them tell you why you are feeling so uncomfortable.

*Listen to your senses.* Give them what is good for them. Look at beautiful things. Listen to beautiful music. Feel softness. If no one else is there to stroke your arm, stroke your own arm. Eat good food. Smell grass, or perfume, or clean laundry. *Make the place where you live as beautiful as you can.* This does not mean spending money on interior decoration. It means quite the opposite. Spending money is one of the main ways in which Americans reinforce their Idealized Selves and distract themselves from their pain. Make beauty from what is around you, creating it yourself. The first thing is often to clean your home and make it tidy, not because cleanliness is next to godliness, but because a clean home is more restful. People often feel anxious when they look around and see a messy home. Organizing things will usually help you to feel better.

Another enjoyable thing that we can do for our senses and our emotions is to make things. Women have done handwork—knitting, embroidery, quilting—from time immemorial. There are many ways of creating: making furniture, carving, gardening.

There is enormous pleasure both in the process of creating and in enjoyment of the product. Just watch out for the temptation to spend money to set yourself up with the equipment that you tell yourself that you must have in order to do something, substituting the process of spending for the process of creating.

# Your Changing Desires

*As you satisfy your desires, they will begin to change.* You may be surprised to find your taste in food changing as you enjoy more complex flavors. Avoid the trap of telling yourself that you don't love chocolate any more, you love sushi, when in fact you still want chocolate. *Be kind to yourself and listen to your emotions.* You may find yourself flipping back and forth in your tastes. That you enjoy sushi one day doesn't mean that you have to enjoy it forever. Listen to your emotions as they tell you *what you really want at that particular moment.*

As our desires develop, we need to give them the opportunity to experience more complex satisfactions. We need to help the desires to develop within the context of our relationship with God and other human beings. That is one reason we traditionally celebrate holidays with good things. For example, for many centuries, small children connected the enjoyment of Christmas sweets and presents with the enjoyment of God. For children, God was sweet and loving because he was part of their experience of sweet things to eat and gifts given to them in love. They also experienced God in the traditional decorations and music.

Later, as they grew up, they understood that God was more than the gifts, the candy, and the decorations, but *they were able to feel God's sweetness, kindness, and beauty through their childhood enjoyment of Christmas.* Adults who had received these joyful things as children could find joy in preparing them and giving them to their own children, in the true meaning of the season, and in the food, companionship, and beauty of the holidays. In this way, *the joys of the body and the joys of the spirit were united in the experience of God's goodness.*

As you begin to experience goodness with your senses, *you need to watch for the feeling that nothing can change for the better.* Your emotions have suffered for many years. When you were young, your feelings of hope were disappointed again and again. When people experience constant disappointment, they come to expect bad things. This expectation hardens into an inability to experience good things for fear that the good things will be taken away or immediately followed by more bad things. It seems safer not to experience anything good.

You may also be afraid to experience goodness with your senses because you were taught that the senses lead us astray. The opposite is true. God created our senses to show us the beauty and goodness that lead us to him. When our senses are not allowed to experience goodness and beauty, our emotions drive us to find satisfaction in the sensations of fun and excitement.

*It is important to notice good feelings.* When you enjoy eating something, say to yourself, "I am enjoying this." When you see something beautiful, think to yourself, "I'm enjoying looking at this." Notice when you enjoy music or the smell of baking bread. Make opportunities to enjoy simple pleasures. Our greatest joy comes from the pleasures of ordinary life. As a young boy, Jim heard someone say, "If the simple pleasures do not satisfy, what will? And if they are not simple, are they still pleasures?" Jim hasn't been able to find the source of this statement, but he has thought of it often over the years.

# 14
# Educating Your Humane Emotions

As you nurture your senses, you also need to educate your emotions. You need to experience people being kind to each other, doing good things, and dealing constructively with things that hurt them. You may find yourself surrounded by people who are filled with hostility. How can you show your emotions what is good and beautiful?

*One purpose of art, music, and literature is to integrate the mind, the heart, and the senses to make us whole.* When we listen to music, look at something beautiful, or read an edifying story, we use all the abilities of our human nature and give them practice in working together in harmony. One of the best ways to nurture the pleasure emotions as they develop into the humane emotions is to surround ourselves with beautiful art and music. Their beauty is pleasing to the senses and their deeper meaning encourages the growth of our emotions, our intellect, and our will.

There are many different forms of art and music. Classical music, folk music, bluegrass music. Prints of the great painters, folk art, pictures cut from magazines. All of these nurture our senses and emotions. It is good to begin surrounding ourselves with the art and music we most enjoy and find most uplifting. It is also helpful to give our emotions the opportunity to enjoy art and music we may not be familiar with. It is also good to create our own art or music, to draw or to sing around the house. There are many ways of creating beauty—painting, woodworking, playing an instrument, or gardening.

*The Idealized Self is likely to try to hijack any attempt we make to create our own beauty.* It loves to tell us that what we are doing is not good enough. It whispers that our drawings are childish, our voice is terrible. Pay no attention to the Idealized Self. G. K. Chesterton once said that anything worth doing is worth doing badly. When we begin to do something because we love it, we need to allow ourselves to do it without passing judgment on the results. The Idealized Self loves to compare what we do with what the experts have done. We tend to think we have no right to do something unless we plan to do it professionally, or at least well enough to be featured in the local newspaper. This is the Idealized Self telling us that unless we are doing something in order to impress others, we have no right to do it. When we do something because we love to do it, God is pleased.

Human beings have been given another great gift. *We can read.* We can put ourselves in the presence of what is good and beautiful even if our surroundings are stressful and ugly. We can learn about love and goodness by entering into worlds created for us by other people's imaginations.

What is best for us to read? Popular literature tends to pander to the Idealized Self. It presents us with a fantasy world in which the destructive defenses of the Idealized Self seem to work. That is why the popular literature of one era can seem so silly to a later time. The Idealized Self of one era is different from the Idealized Self of another era. It is easy for us to lose ourselves in contemporary stories where the characters gain wealth and power or face dangerous situations and come out victorious. These stories can be fun, but they convey the wrong idea to our emotions, the idea that the Idealized Self will succeed. These books can seem gratifying as we read them, but the momentary satisfaction that we gain from soothing the Idealized Self does not touch our real pain.

# Nurturing Our Emotions through Literature

Other stories, often called great literature, tell us about real emotions. Great literature can be daunting. Many people have picked up *War and Peace,* determined to wade through it, only to quit on page three. The settings of some novels are so alien that we spend all our time trying to keep the names of the characters straight and our emotions do not become engaged with the story.

We may also have avoided literature because much literature in the past half century has been full of ugliness and despair. Novels and short stories present miserable people living meaningless lives. Or they tell the story of a young person escaping the tyranny and foolishness of his parents to find meaning in art. Some modern literature suggests that the Idealized Self is superior when it makes fun of others' beliefs and courageously believes in nothing. Other modern literature suggests that being creative makes an Idealized Self superior to others. These stories also pander to the Idealized Self. If you begin a book and find it depressing or offensive, even if others have praised it as good literature, ask yourself why you are uncomfortable. Chances are that you will find an Idealized Self at work in the book.

You may also find yourself uncomfortable reading Dickens or Dostoevsky. The emotions in great literature may be more mature and complex than you can engage with. If your emotions were not satisfied when you were young, you need to return to the emotions that are most real to you, the emotions that a child feels. The best place to begin is often in the children's section of the public library. There are many beautiful picture books. Take them home and look at them. You can satisfy your longing for beauty as well as satisfy your emotions. There are thousands of children's books. Classics like *Winnie the Pooh, The Wind in the Willows,* and *The Narnia Chronicles* take you into worlds where there are love, kindness, and goodness, and where there are problems suited to the emotional lives of children. When you put yourself in these worlds, you educate your emotions in a kind and loving way.

Wander around the library and let your eyes roam. Often a book will draw your attention because it can help you at a particular point in your growth. If you can, talk to people about the books you are reading. Reading to your own children or grandchildren is the best way to share these emotions and enrich your life and theirs.

Some children's books are distressing. They may claim to help children deal with bad situations, but they are ugly and hostile. If you find a book offensive, or if you find it depressing, don't read it. You are in charge of educating your own emotions, and you have the right to determine what you find good and beautiful. Before you put the book aside, however, ask yourself whether you find the book offensive or whether it might distress you because you see your own hurt and sorrow reflected in the book. Consider this carefully, but if you find the book offensive, don't read it.

Poetry can heal and nurture our emotions. Poetry combines a profound understanding of human life with the pleasures of rhythm and rhyme. There is an enormous store of beautiful poetry from *Beowulf* to modern poets like W. H. Auden, Robert Frost, and Dana Gioia. It is often good to begin with children's poetry, and there are many wonderful poetry books in the children's section of any library. Memorizing poetry nurtures our humane emotions. The poems we memorize become an intimate part of us. If we are stuck in traffic or in line at the bank, we can turn the wait into an opportunity to nurture our real self by silently reciting poetry to ourselves.

## Protecting Our Emotions

Some modern poetry wallows in misery and ugliness. If a poem is offensive, don't read it. *No matter what anyone says, if we assault our senses and emotions with what is ugly and hostile, we are educating ourselves to tolerate what is bad.* As the poet Alexander Pope wrote (emphasis added):

> Vice is a monster of so frightful mien,
> As to be hated needs but to be seen;
> Yet seen too oft, familiar with her face,
> *We first endure, then pity, then embrace.*

If we constantly subject ourselves to what is repugnant, ugly, offensive, or distressing, we allow these things to become integrated into what we are, and we do great damage to ourselves. *What we watch on television or in the movies, the music that we listen to, the pictures we look at, the books that we read all become part of our minds and our hearts, part of our being.* It is better not to watch violent movies or television programs. It is better not to listen to music that grates on our nerves. It is better not to be near things that offend us.

There is art, however, that expresses an objection to what is evil. The indignation expressed in this art is directed not at the viewer, but at social ills. The art of George Grosz and the Dadaists is among these works. While this is great art, it may not be helpful for you to be involved with it when you are struggling with your own personal resentment.

Some contemporary art is simply a way for an artist to throw his own feelings of hurt and resentment into the viewer's face. If we object to the ugliness, we are often accused of being a prude, denying reality, or not being able to appreciate art. The truth is that these works are often hostile, intended to hurt and offend. The best response is not to fight with these artists, which keeps us engaged with them and lets them continue to hurt us, but rather to withdraw from them, not allowing their ugliness to become part of us.

Sometimes, though, we are flooded with feelings of distress and sorrow. Many composers have written beautiful music expressing great sorrow—Mozart's *Requiem,* for example. Many paintings portray sorrow and suffering without being filled with resentment and hostility. Much great literature portrays sorrow and suffering in a truly ennobling way. When we put ourselves in the presence of these works of art, we can feel our sorrow and find ways to integrate these feelings and unite them with what is beautiful and good. This art speaks to our sorrow and suffering without falling into hate, ugliness, or despair.

# Reaching Out for Love

As you begin to grow emotionally, you will find yourself reaching out for the love that you did not receive as a child. *As you reach out, you need to use your intellect to guide this need for love.* All too often, people who have never experienced love reach out in ways that are hurtful to themselves and others. The needs we feel are those of young children, and when we try to satisfy them in an adult context, it can lead to great suffering.

For instance, many people have turned to sexual or romantic relationships to satisfy these needs. At first, in the intensity of romantic and sexual union, this can feel wonderful. But if our needs are those of a small child, they cannot stand up to the demands of an adult relationship. Our partner can tire of trying to meet needs that seem inappropriate and excessive, and the relationship can end in misery and shame.

We need to find safe and appropriate places to receive the love we need. This could be in the context of friendships. It could be in the context of counseling or therapy. It could be in the context of a sports team or volunteer work. It could be in the context of church.

As we begin to mature emotionally, *we need to understand the various stages of growing up and the problems of each stage.* If we are struggling with the feelings common to children between the ages of six and twelve, with the intense longing for friendships with someone of the same sex, we can find ourselves embroiled in fights and cliques that resemble a nine-year-old's social life. This may be appropriate for the school ground. It causes trouble in the context of a women's softball team or a men's Bible study group. We have to be aware of our feelings and guide them with our intellect. One of the best ways to do this is to read books about child development. We can identify, for example, the intense jealousy that we may feel when someone we care about has lunch with another person and recognize it as part of our normal emotional growth. Then we can talk to ourselves or to someone else about these feelings and avoid acting out the feelings.

*We need to avoid becoming overly involved in activities as we reach out to others.* Our Idealized Self is ready to jump into action to earn the love and admiration of those around us. We need to protect ourselves and allow ourselves to receive the nurture that a group can give, assuring those who would press us into service that we will serve when we feel ready to do so.

*One of the most important things we can do is to worship and praise God.* We need to find a place to worship where we can feel comfortable. Churches differ widely, even within denominations, in worship, music, and prayer. We need to find a church where we feel God's presence and where we can enjoy the worship. We need to feed our love of God every day. It is good to begin and end every day with the prayers we are most comfortable with. In addition, an enormous wealth of music, art, and literature has been created over many centuries and in many cultures in the worship of God. We need to bring these into our lives.

As we nurture our pleasure emotions and integrate them with our intuitive intellect and loving will, we need to remember what St. Paul said. "Finally, beloved, whatever is true, whatever is honorable, whatever is just, whatever is pure, whatever is pleasing, whatever is commendable, if there is any excellence and if there is anything worthy of praise, think about these things" (Phil 4:8).

# 15
# Creativity and Morality

As we talk about nurturing our humane emotions, we need to address a serious question. One of the major arguments in modern culture is between those who believe that creativity is the central focus of life and those who believe that morality is central. The advocates of creativity caricature those who emphasize morality as repressive and repressed. Those who emphasize morality view the other side as dissolute and irresponsible. To settle this quarrel, we need to understand how creativity and morality are related.

First, we need to explore some assumptions underlying this disagreement. Traditionally art was considered one of the best ways to teach, since art combines both learning and pleasure. We tend to remember the words to songs we learned when we were young long after we've forgotten grammar lessons. Art—pictures, stories, poems, or songs—helps us to comprehend the meaning of things. Art can help us to engage with the spiritual world. It can help us to mature. It can create a bond among those who experience it. Art can also serve to refine the pleasure emotions and to integrate them with our intellect and will.

We have all experienced this. For example, there is an indescribable feeling of oneness that sometimes takes hold of people who are singing or playing music together. There is the thrill of hearing a really good band play. Or the joy of seeing a painting that moves us deeply. If we love the works of a certain author, we feel at one with him. We may even be amazed, if we meet him, to discover that he doesn't know us, because he has understood our feelings so well.

Artists were once regarded as members of a community who had a gift of intuiting the community's deepest feelings and communicating them back to others in a beautiful and skillful manner. This united the individuals in the community and gave them pleasure both in being understood and in being at one with others.

At some point, ideas about art and artists changed. The idea of the "genius" came into being. People tend to think of a genius as an individual who is uniquely endowed with a creative talent. This talent supposedly comes from within the individual, not from God or from the community. Because of his individual talent, the genius may feel that he is not bound by the obligations that bind other community members. He may feel that he is special. Indeed, the genius has become a special form of the Idealized Self.

An artist's Idealized Self may see itself soaring far above the mundane world, above the petty rules and cares of other people. Creativity can then become an excuse for bad behavior. The genius may feel that he can use people to further his own greatness, and that the greatness of his Idealized Self justifies whatever harm he might cause by exploiting those he sees as lesser beings.

Art also becomes a way for artists to express their hostility. We can see this in works of art that "challenge" the viewer, and in the pleasure that many artists take in upsetting and insulting people they perceive as mundane or stupid. Creativity is thus equated with hurting. Any art that aims to please is looked down on as saccharine or insincere. Far from uniting, this kind of art becomes a medium of hostility and division.

## Christian Morality and Utilitarian Morality

The rise of the genius came about as the world was split into matter and spirit by the philosophers of the Enlightenment. Creativity was supposed to come from the higher world of the spirit, cut off from the mundane material world of science and industry, which was controlled by unchanging and unchangeable laws of nature.

At the same time, those in science and industry saw themselves as dealing with the real world, a world that could be measured, controlled, and directed. One part of the world that those in industry often hoped to measure, control, and direct was other human beings. Human beings became Human Resources, comparable to coal, railroads, or machines. Industrialists hoped that human energy could be controlled and directed with the same efficiency as the energy of water power or electricity.

It turned out that human beings were much less cooperative than electricity, much less predictable, and much more likely to decide on any given day that they didn't feel like working. Human beings also got into all kinds of trouble that machines did not—sex, violence, and demands for better working conditions. In response to all this "bad behavior," morality became a strategy for controlling human behavior so that it would be more predictable and useful.

This utilitarian morality differs from Christian morality. Christian morality aims at the perfection of each person within the community of the kingdom of God. Utilitarian morality aims at creating orderly and productive individuals within the economy and the nation. Those who want people to be moral often mean that they want others to work hard and be orderly, while they see themselves as special and entitled to exploit others. Because those who support utilitarian morality often do so in the name of Christianity, many people do not realize that they do not have to reject Christian morality when they reject utilitarian morality.

Preachers aid in this confusion when they encourage moral behavior based on the pragmatic idea that the most important thing is to be useful and well-behaved. Despite all the quarrels over faith and works, we are often encouraged to be religious so that we can help others and impress them with our goodness. We are not encouraged to pray because we are God's children and he loves to talk with us. We are told to pray because it is our obligation or because it is the way to receive the blessings of wealth and well-being. Morality is too often defined in Christian churches in purely pragmatic, utilitarian terms.

Morality is not about being useful and well-behaved. This is the morality of the Idealized Self, trying to earn God's love and the love of those around us. Christian morality grows out of being a child of God, loving and desiring what is good. As we respond to God's unfathomable love, we perceive God's goodness. Then we can desire that goodness and order our lives so that we can experience the joy of being God's children and sharing God's love with his other children. The purpose of morality is not to be good or useful. *The purpose of morality is love.* "You shall love the Lord your God with all your heart, and with all your soul, and with all your mind. This is the greatest and first commandment. And the second is like it: You shall love your neighbor as yourself" (Matt 22:37–39).

## Morality and Creativity

An important part of love is creativity. Creativity is one way human beings love the material world and unite themselves with it. It is an essential part of being human, whether it involves planting a garden, inventing a tool, or choosing a birthday present. Unless people are driven by the Idealized Self, they create out of love and enjoyment. Love and enjoyment move them to learn and perfect an activity, whether it is building a bookcase or singing a song. Then, as they master the activity, they want to try new ways of building or singing. Creativity is also one way in which human beings unite themselves with others. People who sing or tell stories together feel united in a way that people who watch television together do not.

Creativity involves morality. If we allow ourselves to act on our emotions without understanding them, we can act in ways that give destructive emotions a concrete existence in the world. For instance, some people claim that guns do not kill people, that people kill people. This is true. But it is also true that when the assault weapon was created, it was given reality in the material world out of someone's desire to kill someone else. Someone created an efficient means to kill out of his desire to kill or out of his desire to make a profit by selling the weapon to someone else who wanted to kill. Once someone had created a more efficient means of killing, anyone who desired to act out his hostility had a better means to do so.

This is also true of hostile music, painting, or stories. Once hostile art has been created, it continues to cause harm. Hostile movies or stories encourage those who are full of hostility, rage, and resentment to wallow in those emotions and to act them out rather than trying to understand them. This hostile behavior also hurts the artist, cutting him off from others and encouraging him to believe that it is acceptable to hurt others.

On the other hand, when we act out of love, what we create brings forth God's goodness in the material world. The music of Mozart and Bill Monroe, the paintings of Monet and Yuri Gorbachev, the stories of Dickens and Flannery O'Connor can teach us about goodness and lead us to desire what is truly good.

Morality also involves creativity. Human beings were created to be God's stewards in the world. We have to make decisions every day about what might be the optimum good in many situations. We decide what to fix for dinner. We decide what plants to put in front of the house. We decide what to do when faced with other people's bad behavior. In each case, we must understand and respect the nature that God has given to each part of the world and to each thing in it so that we can act, not just according to a rule, but out of love. "For the letter kills, but the Spirit gives life" (2 Cor 3:6). Knowing what to choose and how to act to bring about goodness in the world is creativity at its highest.

Morality and creativity are at heart inseparable. Morality without creativity can be dead. Creativity without morality can be destructive. Each can be empty without the other. Each perfects the other in love. Both are part of the kingdom of God.

# 16
# Habits: The Bones of Life

Habit is one of the best tools for integrating the heart and the mind. Habit gets a bad press these days. Many view it as the opposite of creativity and spontaneity. They claim that it makes us dull and rigid. *But habit is a source of strength, a support for creativity.* For instance, the ability to read is a habit. At first it is hard to do and it is not much fun. A child cannot spend much time thinking about the story because she is struggling to sound out the words. Later, when the habit is fully formed, she can forget about the mechanics and enjoy the story.

Athletes spend hours developing habits of proper performance. Then in the excitement of the game, their bodies know just what to do. Michael Jordan doesn't have to think, "Now, dribble. Turn. Don't travel." All this is so much a habit that he can concentrate on strategy.

Habit frees our attention for more interesting things than the mechanics of living. It also prepares us for emergencies. Habit makes our responses so much a part of us that we don't have to think about each step of what we do. As a child grows and learns to guide her emotions with her intellect and will, she develops the habit of guiding them. For instance, if a child regularly refrains from eating junk food, she develops the habit of eating good food. Then, when faced with chips or a soda, she is able to decide whether or not she really wants to eat them under the circumstances, and she can choose not to eat them without feeling conflicted or deprived.

If we have developed the habit of letting our intellect and will guide our emotions, we can be free of a great deal of turmoil. For instance, think of the distress that many people feel when they must change their diet after a heart attack. Because they are in the habit of eating rich food whenever the desire arises, when they must forgo the immediate sensual good of rich food for the better good of health, the desire for rich food rebels. The desire is not used to being guided, and it does not want to start now. The conflict between the desire for a sensual good and the desire for a more abstract good can be very unpleasant if we have not integrated our desires with our intellect and will and become accustomed to their working together.

The architect Christopher Alexander has studied how people live their lives within their homes and towns. He writes that people's lives can be described in terms of about twelve patterns. That is, each person has approximately twelve clusters of activities that define the greater part of her life. For instance, there is the *getting-up pattern*. Some people sleep as late as possible, throw everything together catch-as-catch-can, and rush distractedly out the door. Others may get up early, drink a cup of coffee, take a shower, and leave for work a few minutes before traffic gets heavy.

There are also *evening patterns*—throwing a frozen dinner into the microwave and watching the news, or supervising the kids' homework while pulling a Quick and Easy recipe from a magazine. Saturday morning patterns can include shopping for food and running the kids to lessons or heading for the lake.

Alexander points out that these patterns are, to a large extent, the shape of our lives. They are our habits, the structure on which the rest of our life rests. *Life is what we do every day. Our habits determine whether we will find everyday life painful or joyful.* If we develop habits that support what we desire, we free enormous energy that would otherwise go into everyday decisions, and we can then direct that energy into love and creativity.

## Using Habit to Defend Our Feelings

Some call habit the enemy of feeling. *It is more accurate to call habit the defender of feeling.* Our emotions change because they respond to what we perceive in the material world. If our daily world is chaotic, stressful, or ugly, our emotions will tell us loud and clear that all is not right. That is their job and they are going to do it. If, on the other hand, we can use habit to create an environment for ourselves that is peaceful and beautiful, our emotions will respond. Many people live in situations that are ugly and chaotic, but we are free to change what we can, one step at a time.

*Our habitual will is a collection of habits.* We can change our habitual will to reflect our free will by *taking tiny steps and making small compromises.* It is overwhelming to think of never again eating sweets. We can say to ourselves, "I can have a piece of cake this evening. Right now I won't."

As we take each small step, we need to stop and notice that we feel better. We have emotional habits as well as habits of living. We feel bad partly because we are used to feeling bad, and we tend to notice the things around us that reinforce our bad feelings. When we say this, we are not saying that you should just cheer up. That demand comes from the Idealized Self. When our real self is suffering, trying to cheer up just makes the suffering worse. But if we allow the real self to enjoy the things we do to relieve its suffering, we will begin to feel better without trying to force ourselves into false cheer. *It is important to notice each improvement. If we do not, we can often feel as bad as if we had not made it.*

The first step in changing our patterns is to stop and look at them. Life is what occurs while we are waiting for something to happen. The Idealized Self whispers to us that soon some really big thing will happen that will change everything, and then we will be happy. Jim has heard many patients say, "I thought that when I made a hundred thousand dollars a year or got that new car, THEN I would be happy." In every case the novelty of the money or the car soon wore off and made no difference. Life is what we do every day. The question is, do we find joy in that life?

Habits are the bones of our lives. By themselves they may be dry and lifeless, but we would look pretty funny without them. We need to think about each piece of our lives—how we get up, how we eat, how we spend Saturday morning. What small change could we make that would help us to feel better? One woman found that making her bed every morning made her feel enormously better when she got home from work. One man got up five minutes early to spend time just looking at the morning. *As we do the one thing that can make us feel better, we really do need to stop and experience the pleasure that the change gives us.*

We can also think about the pattern of our spiritual lives. We have all experienced how difficult it is to feel the joy that God has promised us. Once again, habit can be our friend. Over the centuries, people have developed daily habits that have served as spiritual channels through which their emotions could flow— habits of morning and evening prayer, prayer at meals, or talking to God as they carried on their daily tasks. While the emotions did not flow every time a person prayed, the habit of spending time with God became a protected place where joy could spring up. Joy can spring up at any time, but it can go unnoticed as we rush around distractedly.

## Tradition and Habit

Traditions are habits that have lasted for generations. There are those who find habit and tradition oppressive. Oddly enough, *we Americans have one very strong tradition: the tradition of rebellion.* We tend to suspect that everyone around the world would feel the same way we do about tradition if they were allowed to, but it is possible that this tendency to reject what our parents have told us and to find our own way of doing things is a habit that we Americans have formed over the centuries. If we examine American movies, music, stories, and television, we consistently find the picture of hostile or negligent parents oppressing their children until the children escape to a better and richer life. In telling this story again and again, we form in ourselves the habit of rejecting everything that has gone before us, of seeing habit and tradition as restricting and confining instead of as supportive and helpful.

We are encouraged to start our own traditions. But traditions are, by definition, handed down to the next generation. We imagine handing our own new traditions on to our children without realizing that they, too, will want to reject what has gone before and to start their own traditions in the hope of handing them on to their children. Perhaps we might start by reconsidering our parents' traditions.

Habits are the bones of our lives. They are not the flesh and blood of our experience, but they give life shape and meaning. *Habits free us from constant struggle and internal conflict. They create protected spaces in which our humane emotions and our relationship with God can flourish.* With the help of habit, we can create patterns of love and beauty, and we can establish the life that we long to live.

# 17
# Other People's Feelings

We have talked about listening to our own feelings and hearing what they have to tell us, and we have said that our feelings are not bad or wrong. Although they are incomplete, they tell us about something real in the world and in ourselves. But what about other people's feelings? Unfortunately, we often assume that if our feelings are right, another person's feelings must be wrong. For example, your wife feels that you don't pay enough attention to her. You feel overwhelmed by all that you have to do—your job, the kids, the house. How could she expect more of you? Your wife, on the other hand, feels that she does more than her share, cleaning, cooking, and running the kids to their activities, all in addition to her job. She feels let down and overwhelmed. Whose feelings are right?

This is the wrong question. The question is not whose feelings are right and whose feelings are wrong. If the question is asked in this way, the result is simply a power struggle. The whole situation then boils down to a fight to determine whose feelings are right and, therefore, who will win. The winner, the person whose feelings are deemed right, then gets his or her way. But the loser in this struggle is likely to go away convinced that his or her feelings are right and that the other person just wouldn't listen. The power struggle goes on.

The question is not whose feelings are right, but *how* each person's feelings are right. Just as we need to listen to our own feelings and determine what they are really trying to tell us, we need to listen to other people's feelings and *accept them as real and valid.* Instead of asking, "How could anyone feel like that?" it is better to ask, "Why would this person feel that way? *What is right in what this person is saying?*"

Once again, our intellect has an important role to play. In each feeling is a core of truth. The idea is to find that truth and examine it in the light of our understanding. In the case of the husband and wife above, the truth is that both of them are feeling overwhelmed. Both of them are not getting something they need in their daily lives. The next step is not to decide whose fault it is. *Finding fault is not a helpful concept.*

Some people say, "Well, okay. I'm at fault. I'll stuff these feelings into the closet and just be loving and giving." This is not fair to the other person. All you do when you stuff your feelings down is create a larger pool of rage, hostility, resentment, and bitterness.

In fact, you are abdicating your responsibility to the other person. Look at the word *responsibility*. The root of the word is "response." We need to respond to those around us, letting them know how we feel and accepting how they feel. Only in this way can we build real relationships. If we are irritated with someone, for instance, there is a reason. "Reason" implies that there is something to *understand* in the situation, something that goes beyond the irritation. Without worrying about who is at fault, we are called upon to recognize the truth that lies in our own and others' feelings and to examine those feelings with our intellect.

## Accepting Other People's Feelings

How do you accept other people's feelings without denying your own? First of all, remember that it is not a question of whose feelings are right. Instead of figuring out how the other person is wrong, ask yourself, *"In what way are his feelings right?"* Start by listening to what the person is saying without interrupting. Even if the other person is telling you what you have done wrong, do not concentrate on that. Just listen to what he is saying. Try to hear beyond any blame or fault-finding. Do not defend yourself. Do not point out how he is wrong. Do not state your own case. Do not interrupt. Try to figure out what he is experiencing. Is he angry? Hurt? Overwhelmed? Then say, "Boy, you sound like you're hurting," or, "It sounds to me like you're feeling over-whelmed." Express what you understand of the other person's concerns. There is a real reason that he is feeling that way. If you haven't perceived his feelings correctly, he will have a chance to correct you.

Then express your acceptance of his feelings. For example, you can say, "I can see how you would feel that way." With this simple phrase, you accept the other person's feelings and defuse the struggle to determine whose feelings will win. Then, when the other person has had his say, you can answer, "I understand your feelings, but here's the way I'm feeling." Then do not explain how what the other person has said is wrong. Simply state your own feelings. "I feel overwhelmed, too," is a much more helpful response than "You don't have nearly as much to worry about as I have."

If each person accepts the other's feelings as valid, it is pos-sible to stop fighting about whose feelings are right, to begin looking at the reasons for each person's feelings, and to think about what can be done to deal with problems. For example, if a husband and wife are both feeling overwhelmed by responsibili-ties, it is more helpful for both to look at what their Idealized Selves may be doing and at what their real selves need. Then they can think about what will help them to feel better. They can make decisions about time and resources that will make it possible for each to get what he or she truly needs.

## Emotional Boundaries

It is important to understand the problem of *emotional boundaries*. Each person needs to be clear about his or her own feelings. As we listen to other people, we can sometimes feel so overwhelmed by their feelings that we respond with similar feelings, not because this is how we actually feel, but to protect ourselves from their feelings. For example, when someone is full of rage, it is tempting to feel rage in response. Never express rage or resentment just because someone else expresses rage or resentment. This accomplishes nothing except the escalation of hostility and resentment on both sides. If you are feeling overwhelmed by another person's feelings, say so in a quiet, matter-of-fact way.

The emotional boundaries between people can break down in another way. Sharing our feelings with others can be a wonderful experience, but it is important not to take over the other person's feelings. For example, if someone feels indignation at the unjust way someone else has treated him, it is sometimes tempting to respond with our own indignation, taking on his feelings in sympathy as if they were our own. If we allow our own feelings of indignation to be kindled by someone else's indignation, we take away the person's feelings and the emotional boundaries break down. His indignation is his response to what happened to him. We did not experience the injustice. It is better just to accept the feeling. We can do this by remaining calm and saying something like, "Wow, that was really unfair. I can see why you're upset." Then it is clear that his indignation remains his and the emotional boundaries remain firm. It is also clear that you have accepted his feelings.

# Denying Other People's Feelings

Another problem is *denying other people's feelings.* We do this in many ways without even thinking. We tell someone, "It wasn't that bad," or "You're just overreacting," or "Think about how the other person felt," or "You really shouldn't feel that way," or "I don't understand how anyone could feel that way." These are all ways of denying the other person's feelings. To deny someone's feelings is to deny his very perceptions of the world, to deny the core of who he is. For example, we may say something like, "There's no need to be so upset. It wasn't that bad." This response says to the other person that you believe that you know better than he does what he should feel in response to what happened to him, or that you are superior to him because you don't feel those feelings. *This is destructive and hurtful.* When someone sees that his feelings are not being accepted, he becomes entrenched in those feelings. It seems to him that to defend his feelings is to defend the very heart of who he is.

We need to respond to other people's feelings neither by denying the reality and importance of the feelings nor by taking over those feelings. We accept other people's feelings by acknowledging the reality and importance of their feelings but remaining firmly within the boundaries of our own feelings. Once we have done that, we may actually have feelings similar to the other person's feelings. For example, we might feel indignation at the injustice the other person experienced. But these feelings would be our own.

*We may deny someone else's feelings because we are afraid of the same feelings in ourselves.* For example, a person with a self-denying neurosis may tell someone who feels resentful that he should not feel that way because she is disturbed by her own feelings of resentment.

# Bringing Our Feelings into the Light of the Intellect

The goal of talking about our feelings is to bring them out into the light of the intellect where we can listen to them and examine them. Not all the emotions we feel in a situation are a response to that situation. For example, if someone's parents always ridiculed what he said, he is likely to hear ridicule when someone is just kidding around. If someone has always experienced kidding as a vehicle for hostile feelings, it is difficult for him to perceive loving feelings in teasing. If the person who feels ridiculed can say, "It didn't feel friendly to me when you said that my hair looks like a haystack," she gives the teaser a chance to answer, "Hey, I was just teasing. I love your hair. You wouldn't be you without that cowlick."

All teasing has an aggressive element in it. It is a way of wrapping in love an observation that might not entirely please the other person. It is also a way of dealing with feelings that we're not entirely comfortable with and maintaining boundaries that we're not sure of. For instance, if an uncle notices that his niece is growing into a lovely young woman, he must treat her neither like a child nor like a sexually available woman. So he teases her, diffusing the feelings and expressing his affection while maintaining the proper boundaries.

But the aggressive element in teasing can get out of hand and become a vehicle for hostility. If someone can say that her feelings are hurt, the other person can take a look at his feelings to see if he spoke in hostility or in love. If he sees a hostile edge in his remark, he can apologize.

*This is responsibility, responding to another person with love and respect.* This makes it possible to get beyond fighting about whose feelings are right and to look at all aspects of a situation. In this way, we can understand what we are feeling, which parts of these feelings are old immature ways of feeling that we still carry around, and which parts of the feelings have to do with the current situation. We can express what we really want and need, and we can satisfy those wants and needs in a way that works instead of acting without thinking and ending up in the same old fights. We can change hurtful ways of responding into new ways of responding that bring us closer to each other, while at the same time preserving our proper boundaries with each other.

# PART III

# Troubleshooting

# 18
# Anger and Rage

People use the word *anger* in many different ways. They speak of anger when they mean rage, hostility, resentment, or bitterness. At the time when the New Testament was written, anger had a specific meaning. If a man felt that someone had offended him, he had to exact revenge for this insult to his honor. He kept the memory of the offense smoldering in his heart until he had a chance to harm the offender. When the New Testament instructs us to avoid anger, it does not refer to the feeling of anger that we have described in Chapter 1. It refers to these cultivated feelings of rage and hostility and the need for revenge. Since mistaking rage for anger can cause great emotional confusion and suffering, we have to distinguish carefully between anger on the one hand and rage, hostility, resentment, and bitterness on the other.

A person faced with an immediate threat of harm reacts with anger to protect himself against the harm. Anger itself is straightforward. *If we realize that we are becoming angry, it is a warning that there may be an immediate threat of some kind.*

A child's anger is straightforward. Children feel angry when they can't get what they want or when they have to do something they don't want to do. It is important to let children experience their anger and express it *verbally*. It is also important to help children distinguish between things that really hurt them and things that do not. Parents serve as a child's intellect when he is small, guiding him and showing him that something that may seem bad to him right now is good for him in the long run. A child may experience having to help around the house as hurting him since he would rather play, and he can't yet understand that household chores are done for his own and others' comfort.

You can say to a child, "It is okay for you to feel angry while you tidy up your room. You can gripe and whine. You can mutter that I'm a mean old grump. But you do have to tidy up, and you do have to learn to do it properly, because a tidy room will make you more comfortable." This teaches the child that his feelings of irritation are okay, but that the feelings are not an excuse for failing to do what he needs to do. When the situation is handled this way, the child does not have to repress his anger.

If a child begins to scream or to throw a tantrum, you can say to him, "It is okay to feel angry, and you can tell me that you are angry, but you are not allowed to throw a tantrum, break things, or throw things." If he does not calm down, you can wrap your arms around him in a loving way and hold him tight, helping him to contain his anger, in loving awareness that he needs help in doing this. A child needs to feel his anger and express it in words. He also needs to experience that many of the things that he becomes angry about are not really hurtful but are actually good in the long run. Then he will learn to guide his anger with his own intellect.

# Rage

A baby has no way to protect himself from harm. He can let those around him know that he is in distress, but if a parent chooses to do nothing or if the parent inflicts the harm, intentionally or not, the child is helpless. What happens then?

*Rage forms when anger cannot do its job.* Anger has a direction, a purpose, a specific harm to overcome. If a child must hide his anger from his parents, the anger cannot do its job. It cannot protect the child from harm and the child feels hate and hurt.

Over time, repressed anger joins with the hate and the hurt and turns into rage.

If the harm continues, the feeling of hurt grows and the hate grows with it. As hate builds up, the child begins to perceive the person who is hurting him not just as bad, but as an enemy. This feeling of enmity is called *hostility*. The child also feels indignant at being treated unjustly. This long-term feeling of indignation is called *resentment*. Hostility and resentment grow into a deep-seated ill will toward the person who is causing the hurt, and this ill will is called *bitterness*.

Rage, hostility, resentment, and bitterness are not anger. These feelings are ramifications of hate, and they grow when a child must repress his anger over a long period of time. Because these feelings are the result of so much hurt, *any new experience of hurt is magnified.* It is like Chinese water torture. If a drop of water falls on us, we barely notice it. After many drops, however, each single drop becomes excruciating. *Then the threat of harm no longer arouses anger. It calls forth rage, hostility, resentment, and bitterness.*

Rage, hostility, resentment, and bitterness form a reservoir of bad feelings that eat away at us. Since the Idealized Self cannot bear to admit that the real self feels these feelings, it must project them outward. The Idealized Self can always find something in other people's behavior to justify the rage, hostility, resentment, and bitterness that the real self feels. When we are full of resentment, we are usually extremely aware of anything that is not fair. Some people see things that are not fair to them and feel resentment and bitterness about these things. Some people see things that are not fair to others and channel their hostility and resentment against people or institutions that they see as behaving unfairly. But the resentment and hostility come first, magnifying and coloring the perception of unfairness.

It is important to distinguish between seeing something that really is not fair and wanting to do something about it, and seeing something that is not fair and reacting with resentment and hostility. The former seeks to solve the problem. The latter is destructive both to us and to others because *the hostility and resentment are the driving force and are far less interested in solving the problem than in finding a target for the hostile feelings.*

## Becoming Aware of Your Rage

If you are going to change, you must become aware of your own rage, hostility, resentment, and bitterness. Rage and hostility come dressed in many disguises—irritation, impatience, frustration, indignation. If you are stuck in traffic, notice what you are feeling. If someone does something incorrectly at work, notice what you are feeling. If you can't get a tool or appliance to work, notice what you are feeling. If you see people doing what you consider morally wrong, notice what you are feeling. Especially notice what you are feeling as you read the newspaper or listen to the nightly news.

When you notice that you are feeling rage or hostility, *do not try to stop feeling these emotions.* If you try to make the hostility go away, you are compounding the problem. Simply feel the rage, the hostility, and the resentment. Do not act on them. Put your emotional engine in neutral and feel it roar. The hostility will probably diminish after you listen to it for a while. Large muscle exercise such as walking, running, or working out helps to calm the feelings.

By distinguishing among rage, hostility, resentment, and bitterness you can begin to understand your reactions. When you feel rage, what set it off? When you feel hostile, whom do you perceive to be your enemy? Why? Is that person intentionally trying to harm you? Why do you feel resentment? What injustice are you reacting to? And what about bitterness? What ill will do you feel and toward whom? Why? As you listen to your emotions you can begin to distinguish between the hurt you have suffered in the past and the events in your present life.

## Passive-Aggressive Behavior

Feelings of rage, hostility, resentment, and bitterness often come out not in active attack, but in subtle ways of frustrating others. We've all run into a store clerk who can't or won't find what we're looking for, a workman who just can't seem to get it done right, or a bureaucrat who can't seem to understand what we are talking about. This is hostile behavior expressed not actively, but passively. It is called *passive-aggressive behavior* because it is at the same time passive (after all, no one is really attacking anyone) and aggressive (I'll see that you don't get what you want no matter how hard you try).

It is easy to be aware of this behavior in other people. Many people are passive-aggressive, and when we come across them, we need to be aware of the hostile nature of their behavior. But the key to changing is to *become aware of our own passive-aggressive feelings and behavior.* We express passive-aggressive feelings in forgetfulness, in losing things, in accidentally breaking things, in not understanding what people are saying or what they want, in procrastination, in intentional inefficiency, in withholding significant information, and in making mistakes. Each time you do one of these things, stop and ask yourself what you are feeling.

If you are feeling fuzzy-brained, confused, or lethargic, look more closely at these feelings. Ten to one, rage, hostility, resentment, and bitterness lurk underneath them. Ask yourself what the feelings are about. Do you feel that someone is getting something that you should have? Do you enjoy the power to control the situation? Do you feel that someone is getting something he doesn't deserve? Do you feel that someone is trying to control you?

*Do not think about what someone else is doing. Pay attention to your own feelings of rage, hostility, resentment, or bitterness.* Listen to your emotions. How does the present situation remind you of something that happened to you early in your life? If you can't stop and listen to your emotions right then, bring the situation back into your mind at the end of the day and see what pops into your head. Then really feel *that* situation, the one that your emotions remember.

## The Pleasure of Getting Rid of Rage

But, you say, all of this takes so much time and energy. Yes. It does. It means that you may have to give up some hours of television, golf, or shopping. But consider that television, golf, and shopping could be ways of distracting yourself from these feelings. If you pay attention to the feelings instead of distracting yourself, you will begin to feel better. When you are no longer overwhelmed by rage, hostility, resentment, and bitterness, you will have more energy. Rage, hostility, resentment, and bitterness exhaust us. As you understand your feelings, you can bring them under the influence of your intellect and free yourself from the control that they have over you. You will begin to experience love, desire, and joy. You will enjoy your work more. You will enjoy being with people more. You will be a better parent, less likely to do to your own children the hurtful things that were done to you. You will also sleep better.

Earlier in this chapter we spoke of lovingly wrapping your arms around a child to help him contain his emotions. You need to treat yourself with the same loving kindness. Your rage, hostility, resentment, and bitterness are there for a reason, but they hurt you as much as they hurt others, if not more. Wrap your arms around your feelings, hold them tight, and listen to them. Treat them with love and give them a respectful hearing. After all, underneath those terrible feelings is a terrible hurt. You have to work on the feelings until you can feel the hurt instead of the rage, hostility, resentment, and bitterness. When you can feel the hurt, you will understand how your feelings can change.

# 19
# Anxiety, Worry, and Fear

Anxiety, worry, and nervousness are different kinds of fear. We may feel anxious or worried about money, the future, our children, what people think of us, our job. *The basic emotion is fear.* Whatever we might be worried about, we need to listen to the fear itself, because while we may have problems, *the fear is usually not about these problems.* Stop and think. If you find one problem solved, do you immediately start worrying about something else?

Some people think that we should be afraid of God. "The fear of the Lord is the beginning of wisdom" (Ps 111:10). This word for fear is different from the Hebrew word for the kind of fear that we feel in our daily lives. This expression, therefore, would better be translated into modern English, "Reverence for the Lord is the beginning of wisdom."

*One of the things that people most often fear is their own emotions. The emotions that they most often fear are hate and anger.* If parents want to raise children who feel love and compassion for others, they may react to their children's hate and anger by telling them that they should not feel that way. If they fear their own hate and anger, parents may fear these emotions in their children and withdraw from them emotionally when the children are angry.

Because a child's Idealized Self desperately wants to get rid of her hate and anger to please her parents, she begins to fear these emotions and the reaction that her parents have to them. Soon the child feels only fear. Because the child cannot allow herself to recognize what she is really afraid of—her own hate and anger—*she learns to fear the things that provoke her hate and anger.*

# Getting Rid of Fear

If we want to get rid of our worry, fear, and anxiety, we need to stop when we feel afraid, anxious, or worried and ask ourselves what happened just before we felt this way. There is a very good chance that something aroused our hate, our anger, or both. But because buried hate and anger turn into rage and hostility, what we probably felt was an alarming spurt of rage. Because we were taught that it is wrong to feel rage, we quickly pushed it out of sight. We felt only fear.

*But we fear what we hate and we hate what we fear.* So, whenever we feel fear, it is helpful to ask ourselves why we might be feeling hate. We feel hate when we perceive something bad or potentially harmful. But we also feel fear. When we perceive something hateful, we fear it because it is potentially harmful. When we fear something, we also hate it as something bad. We hate what we fear, and we fear what we hate.

*We are usually more aware of one of these emotions. We are more aware of hate when courage predominates over fear.* Then we may think about what we can do to those we hate. When we think someone has hurt us, our impulse is to get revenge, to return hurt for hurt. That, our emotions tell us, will bring the matter to a close. Everything will be evened up and we will feel better. Unfortunately, the person on whom we take revenge is likely to believe that she then needs to return a hurt for what we have done to her. *When we hate someone, we are afraid of her,* and the fear intensifies the hate.

What if fear predominates over courage? People who are raised to believe that it is wrong to hate generally suppress the hate. Then they not only fear what they hate, they also fear the hate itself. Fear becomes the predominant feeling. To complicate matters, a person may then decide that it is childish or cowardly to feel fear and may decide that she will be courageous. Then courage represses the fear that is repressing the hate.

Unfortunately, the fear cannot get rid of the hate. The hate may leak out around the edges, making us irritable, impatient, or short-tempered. Or we can turn the hate against ourselves, creating depression. Often the Idealized Self projects the hate onto the world around us. Then we see in others the emotions that we fear in ourselves. We may believe that it is others, not we, who are full of hostility. We begin to look for reasons why we should hate and fear someone else—our neighbors, foreigners, the other political party. When we fear something, we need to stop and look at our own feelings. What do we hate in ourselves that arouses such fear in us?

## What We Fear Has Already Happened to Us

When we are overwhelmed with fear, we also need to ask ourselves what might have happened to us in the past that has primed us to be so fearful. *The thing we fear most is often something that has already happened to us, not exactly as we fear it, but in some way that we have not been able to understand.* The intellect, aware of the terrible fear, tries to find an explanation of the fear that sounds reasonable. An example may help to explain this. A young woman was consumed with fear that she was going to die and leave her two little girls motherless. Sometimes she sat for hours overwhelmed by sorrow, imagining how terrible they would feel without her. Soon she was afraid to drive, fearing that she might be killed in an automobile accident.

One day she was talking to a friend about her fear. The friend asked her, "Didn't you lose your own mother when you were little?" Suddenly the woman realized what her fear was about. She had been given up for adoption when she was born, and although her adoptive mother had been a good mother to her, she had felt fear at some very deep level when she lost her birth mother. The memory of that feeling had stayed with her, and since her intellect could not figure out what the feeling actually meant, it had decided that the fear must be about her own children losing their mother. When she realized that the fear was her reaction to her own profound loss, she no longer felt afraid of dying and leaving her own children alone. The thing she feared most had already happened to her. This is usually the case.

To give another example, let us consider a woman who was deathly afraid of earthquakes. She was certain that everything she had would be lost when the "Big One" came. One day she decided to listen to her fear. She recalled the day, when she was five years old, when an ambulance had taken her mother away. Her mother had remained in a mental hospital for several months, and no one had told the girl what was wrong or had allowed her to see her mother. She had been afraid that her mother was dead and that people were afraid to tell her the truth. To a five-year-old child, it felt as if the earth had been shaken to its foundations. Her intellect, seeing her fear many years later, reasoned that only a massive earthquake could cause such a loss.

We hate what we fear and we fear what we hate. What we fear most has already happened to us. When we are overwhelmed with fear, we need to listen to our emotions. These emotions are usually out of proportion to what we experience in the present, but they are not out of proportion to things that have happened to us in the past. Until we listen to the emotions and hear what they are really trying to tell us, we are held captive to what has already happened. We can't experience the world around us in a realistic way. To be free to change, we need to listen to our fear and bring it into the light of the intellect.

# 20
# Depression

You can barely get up in the morning. Love, desire, and joy are words that have no meaning. Only exhaustion and despair remain. Everything overwhelms you. Depression is a terrible burden that you can't carry and you can't put down. Add the guilt: "Why can't I feel better? I'm such a burden to everyone."

There is hope. It is likely that you cannot feel hope, but you can let God lead you out of depression's swamp of despair and misery. If you allow God to lead you, if you let him show you the way step by step, *God will not fail you.* The authors know this. They have been there.

First, the biochemical aspect of depression is real. Because our emotions are part of our bodies, our cells react biochemically when we feel emotions, and these biochemicals are stored in our cells so that the cells will remember how to react to similar situations in the future. In depression, our cells are choked with biochemicals of rage, fear, and misery that have built up over years of being hurt. It is hard for our emotions to speak to us even when we ask them what they have to say because the cells can hardly do more than moan. An antidepressant medication can be very helpful. Often it gives us more flexibility in responding to depression. Then the intellect can help our emotions to heal as our understanding comforts and guides our emotions.

It is clear that many people can work on their feelings more effectively if they take an antidepressant. Some people refuse to take them, claiming that they don't want to depend on a drug. But aspirin is a drug. Penicillin is a drug. *Drugs can help our system to deal* with a problem. *Depression is a serious problem, and an antidepressant medication can give us the margin of strength to deal with it.* "I don't need a crutch," some people announce. But if we have a broken leg, a crutch allows us to keep the weight off our injured leg while it heals. An antidepressant can help take the weight off our battered emotions and give us room to heal. We are not suggesting antidepressants as a cure-all for depression. Your doctor can help you find an appropriate antidepressant medication.

# Why We Feel Depressed

*We feel depressed when our cells believe that nothing we do can make any difference in our lives, that everything is completely hopeless.* Our emotions respond to a possible threat with one of two reactions—fight or flight. We feel either courage or fear. We prepare either to overcome harm or to escape from it. Sometimes, though, we can do neither. If our anger cannot overcome a threat, we have to endure harm. Then the two emotions that sustain us are hope and courage, while our anger remains ready to overcome the harm if the chance arises.

Sometimes there seems to be no way of overcoming harm or escaping from it. Hope and courage fade. Fear wells up. Anger exhausts itself as it rises up time and again to protect us, and time and again is beaten down. Then, all emotional energy exhausted, the cells simply give up. They conclude that nothing they do can makes any difference. They cease to care and they wait for the end.

In the course of working with loving mothers and their babies, researchers asked the mothers on one occasion not to respond when their babies smiled or gurgled at them. The babies all reacted in the same way when their mothers did not respond to them. First, they were startled. They smiled more broadly and gurgled more loudly, reaching out to their mothers. When they received no response, they redoubled their efforts, becoming more and more frantic. Then they became angry, demanding that their mothers smile at them. Finally, still receiving no response, they sank back in misery and despair.

This happened to the babies in the experiment only once, and the breach with their mothers healed quickly. But if the experience happens often, the breach does not heal. At the beginning of the twentieth century, many babies living in orphanages died. Doctors assumed that the cause of these deaths was an infection which they called "marasmus," and researchers set out to find the cause of the infection. Instead, they learned many years later that the infants died from lack of love. They were cared for competently and matter-of-factly by overburdened caregivers who took little time to hold them or talk to them. The infants reached out more and more frantically to those around them, then became angry. When they received no loving response, they sank into depression and died.

If a baby does not feel loved, he does not necessarily die, but he will live with a black hole at the center of his heart that cannot be filled with anything except love. When he grows up, he may look to stimulation for a reason to go on living: excitement, the physical pleasures of eating, then of drugs and partying. He may look desperately for someone to love him, turning from friend to friend and adult to adult. He may appear hostile and resentful.

Eventually the hope and courage that create the Idealized Self can begin to fail. Fear and despair creep in. Nothing seems to work. A child who is full of rage, who desperately needs love, is hard for the average person to cope with, let alone love. Hostility and fear grow as the child can neither fight the situation nor escape from it. The child's Idealized Self hates its unloved and miserable real self, often longing to destroy it. Courage turns to despair.

Sometimes it can take years for this cycle to complete itself. Children are naturally courageous creatures, full of energy and the longing to survive. The natural energy of childhood and youth can help many people to survive into adulthood. But whether in childhood, adolescence, or adulthood, one day a person may begin to realize that nothing matters any more. Nothing, his feelings conclude, will change. All the things he has done to find love have failed. When the emotions come to this conclusion, the intellect and the will lose energy, and the black hole gapes ever larger.

# Turning to God

*But it can change.* Not quickly. Not easily. But it can change. *God can give us the love that we need to survive.* A person who is depressed has a very difficult time feeling God's love for him because he doesn't know what God's love would feel like. You can't describe color to a person born blind, and you can't describe God's love to someone who hasn't experienced human love. If someone has not felt the love that one human being gives another, he will have a very difficult time experiencing God's love.

But God's love is real. In our depression and despair, we must turn to God and ask for that love. But just as a person born blind has to learn to see if surgery gives her sight later in life, so we have to *learn* to feel loved. If we have felt bad for many years, it will take time to learn to feel loved. People may call on God and expect a great blinding burst of love to explode in their hearts. If this doesn't happen, they assume that God hasn't heard them.

An old story tells about a man trapped on his roof in a flood. He asked God to save him. A canoe came by, but the man waved it on. "God will save me," he said. A motorboat came by. "God will save me," called the man. A rowboat came by and called to him.

"Don't worry about me," he called back. "God will save me." The man was swept away by the flood and drowned, and when he appeared before God's throne he asked God, "Why didn't you save me?" "Well," God answered, "how many boats did you want me to send?"

If we ask God for help, he will send a boat, the *one thing we need so that we can take the next small step. If we take that step, God will show us the next step.* God does not usually sweep away troubles and sorrows in one grand gesture. We couldn't bear it if he did. We wouldn't know who we were or what to do next. *Each time we do the one simple thing that is there before us, we are healed as much as we can be healed at that moment.*

This book could be a canoe that God has sent to you. If you read this book and follow its suggestions, you will begin to feel better. But depression can take years to grow. You cannot overcome depression just by reading any book once. You have to keep at it. Read this book over and over. Begin listening to your emotions. Read the books that we list in Chapter 24, especially the books by Karen Horney. Pay attention to what your Idealized Self is doing. *It is especially important to nurture your senses and your pleasure emotions in the ways that we describe in Chapters 13 and 14.* Allow yourself to feel pleasure and to believe that the pleasure is real.

When we are depressed, it is difficult to believe that truth, beauty, and goodness are real. A voice inside of us tells us that the person who is kind to us just feels sorry for us. It whispers that if we feel better when we are listening to beautiful music, it is just for a minute. It whispers that the sense we have of God's presence is just self-delusion. Watch out for the voice that tells you that anything that helps you to feel better is just an illusion. This voice is the voice of the Idealized Self, full of hate for your real self and desperate to maintain its control over you. *This voice will attack you again and again, assuring you that nothing can change, that any change you perceive is a delusion.* This is where your intellect and will can see what the Idealized Self is trying to do, and you can choose not to believe the Idealized Self each time it speaks. You might tell the Idealized Self that you appreciate all that it has done for you, but it can be quiet now.

*One of the Idealized Self's tricks is to tell you that the next simple step is stupid, that it is too small to do any good, that it won't work.* Taking each step as it presents itself is called faith. The emotion that keeps us going step by step is hope. The end toward which we are moving is love. These three things remain—faith, hope, love. God *will* lead you step by step.

# 21
# Sex

Sex. There it is. Not that it wasn't there before, but ever since Freud suggested that sexuality stands at the center of what moves us, the uproar hasn't stopped. And he was right as far as he went. Freud's ideas about sexuality were a profound insight into the nature of human emotions, but the total context of Freud's insight has been lost.

The truth is that *sex stands at the center of what moves us because love, desire, and pleasure stand at the center of what moves us. Because we are made to live in the material world, our emotions of love, desire, and pleasure have a powerful and irreducible physical element.* From the moment we are born, we want to know other people in a physical way. Babies want to be held and cuddled. Young children cling to their mothers. Older children are very physical in their affections, young girls holding hands, young boys wrestling and punching each other. In most cultures around the world, grown men and women walk down the street arm in arm with their friends, embrace when they meet, and sit close together. Adult sexual activity is one manifestation of this physical way of knowing those we love.

Sexual feelings are incredibly powerful. After all, in the first chapter of Genesis, the first thing that God did after he created man and woman was to bless them and tell them to be fruitful and increase in number. Despite some attempts to claim that sexual desire is a result of the fall, it is much more likely that a loving God created man and woman in such a way that they would find great pleasure in what he commanded them to do. The Bible speaks over and over again of sex as a way of knowing, of becoming one with another person. When we unite ourselves with someone sexually, we are not just uniting ourselves with that person physically. We are also uniting ourselves with that person spiritually, whether we perceive it or not.

Many people have claimed that we should look to animals as our model of "natural" sex. But although we are animals, we are not just animals. We share in God's image, and this fact changes the whole nature of our sexual being. What we do on a physical level affects our spiritual being, and our spiritual being affects our physical being. We share only part of our sexual nature with the animals, the instinctual part.

What are we to do with these powerful feelings of desire and pleasure that have become as disordered as the rest of our desires? Sex has created so many problems in our lives that people are often distrustful of it. How many sermons, while giving brief lip service to the goodness of sex in the right context, tell people that their actual sexual feelings are bad? In reaction to this, others have pointed out how good sex is and assumed that those who emphasize the problems must be repressed and ugly-minded. Christians tend to cast discussions about sex in terms of what is sinful and what is not sinful. It is clear that there is sexual behavior that is destructive to our human nature, but when we focus only on the question of sin, we limit our ability to understand what underlies our sexual problems. Once again, we must look at the total context of our lives.

Sexual desire is one aspect of our pleasure emotions, although a very powerful one. Ideally, the pleasure emotions develop into the humane emotions and are integrated with the contemplative intellect and the loving will. But if a child does not experience love, including physical affection, this integration does not take place. Then the total context of adult sexuality is lost, and *sex, by default, becomes the focus of desire. A person who has not experienced love turns to sensation for the satisfaction of the pleasure emotions.* One of the most intense sensations for human beings is sex. Because love, desire, and pleasure are the foundation of our emotional lives, these emotions *do not go away.* These emotions were created to keep us alive and to draw us to what is good for us. If our pleasure emotions have not been able to develop and become integrated with the rest of us, we can find ourselves overwhelmed by our desire for pleasurable sensations, especially the sensations of sex. We may have been told to use our will power to make these desires go away, but we cannot make our desire for pleasure, including sexual pleasure, go away. What we can do is listen to our sexual desires, just as we listen to our other emotions.

## Listening to Our Sexual Desires

We may prefer not to listen to our sexual desires because many of us are ashamed of our sexual feelings and fantasies. We are afraid of what they might tell us about who we really are and what we really feel and desire. *Our sexual desires and fantasies are a window into our deepest emotions.* If we can learn to understand them, we can begin to integrate our sexual feelings into the total context of who we are. We can also find greater pleasure in our sexual lives as our feelings of fear and guilt about these feelings diminish. Dr. Michael Bader's book *Arousal: The Secret Logic of Sexual Fantasies* is an excellent resource for learning to listen to our sexual desires.

We have described how our pragmatic emotions defend our pleasure emotions. Because sexual desires are so powerful and necessary for the survival of the human race, our pragmatic emotions must try to overcome feelings that interfere with sexual desire. Feelings of shame, guilt, and being unloved often arise when we begin to experience sexual desire. Then, just as our imagination and pragmatic emotions try to overcome the pain of feeling unloved, our imagination and pragmatic emotions try to deal with the feelings that stand in the way of sexual desire. They do this through sexual fantasy.

Dr. Bader points out that in sexual fantasy *the imagination creates a story in which the feelings that interfere with sexual desire go away for a while and we feel safe enough to allow sexual feelings to grow.* That is why sexual fantasies are so compelling. Sexual fantasy changes the feelings that interfere with sexual pleasure into feelings that encourage sexual pleasure. The sexual stories the imagination creates reflect our deepest fears and desires. At some level we are aware of this. *Often our sexual fantasies embarrass us because they speak to us of a part of ourselves that the Idealized Self is determined to deny.*

If we examine our sexual fantasies, we can understand the feelings that our sexual problems are trying to tell us about, and we can loosen the grip of compulsive sexual behavior. At the same time, we can understand the problems that many couples have in their sexual relationships and how they can become more comfortable with their sexual desires.

First of all, we need to recognize that *our sexual feelings are not telling us only about our sexual desires. Our sexual feelings are also trying to tell us about our many other needs and desires. If the purpose of sexual fantasies is to overcome the feelings that get in the way of our sexual desires, these fantasies can help us to understand the feelings that get in the way of all of our desires.*

## The Feelings We Bring with Us

Children desire their parents' love more than anything else. If they do not feel loved, the Idealized Self will emphasize some feelings and bury other feelings as it tries to earn the parents' love. We carry these patterns of feeling into our adult relationships as we establish our own families. After all, it was in growing up with our own parents that we learned what to expect from marriage and a family.

One of the things we have to do in understanding our sexual feelings is to understand what our parents wanted from us. *We tend to believe that our spouses want from us what our parents wanted from us.* We are romantically drawn to people whose feelings in some way dovetail with our own family's feelings. *But what we expect our spouses to want from us may not be what they really do want.* Since our spouses also had parents who expected things from them, our spouses often experience us as being like their parents. The bedroom is full of expectations that stand in the way of our sexual impulses.

The variety of sexual fantasies and feelings is enormous, and we can understand a particular person's fantasies only by knowing her particular feelings. But there are some basic patterns that can guide us as we explore our own sexual feelings. Certain kinds of problems appear again and again, and if we look at them, we can get some insight into our own feelings. Dr. Bader describes several of these problems.

## Shame

One of the most common problems is the feeling of shame, of being unlovable, rejected, defective, not good enough. If a child does not feel loved, she always assumes that it is her own fault, that she is not lovable. As adults we may struggle against this assumption, but parents' feelings define reality for their children. We always internalize our parents' feelings, no matter how many times we tell ourselves that their feelings were wrong.

Everyone feels rejected at some time, but the experience of rejection may be so overwhelming that a person is dominated by feelings of shame and worthlessness. These feelings may take the form of feeling ugly, dirty, stupid, or fat. Often people who feel this way do not take care of themselves, or they put on weight because they have no hope of ever feeling attractive or lovable. On the other hand, some people go to the opposite extreme and become obsessed with being perfectly groomed, perfectly thin, perfectly dressed.

Because feelings of shame and rejection are so common, many sexual fantasies create a story about being so lovable that others cannot resist us. These fantasies are common among women. In these fantasies others are helpless when they see our body and the sexuality that our body radiates. Some people assume that these exhibitionistic fantasies represent feelings of self-confidence, but just the opposite is true. Many popular books present the hero or heroine as irresistible to the opposite sex. Our imaginations create a story that turns our feelings of being rejected into feelings of being desirable, and this fantasy allows our sexual desire to grow.

## Guilt

Guilt is another feeling commonly associated with sexual desires. This feeling of guilt has nothing to do with having done something wrong. *This feeling of guilt assumes that our desires themselves will somehow hurt someone.* The fear that someone we love is fragile or easily hurt often accompanies this guilt. Many people feel that they are betraying their parents if they are happier or more successful than their parents are. We may see our parents as weak or vulnerable and feel that we must protect and care for them. We may also fear our parents' envy and resentment. This can be a form of survivor guilt. "My parents didn't make it. For me to make it would be to desert and betray them."

These feelings may include a sense that we hurt our parents when we have more than they had or experience more sexual pleasure than they did. Often we are not even conscious of this feeling of guilt at "getting above our raising." We may feel that it is wrong to have a life of our own. When we carry these feelings of guilt, we may be romantically drawn to people we perceive as weak or sad, hoping that we can make them feel better, just as we tried to make our parents feel better.

There are many fantasies that serve to counteract these feelings of guilt. These include fantasies of being forced to have sex, of secret sex, of pretending to be innocent while carrying out a secret sexual relationship, or of defying authority by having sex. All of these scenarios create a world in which it is okay to feel sexual pleasure without guilt.

We bring our shame and guilt into our sexual relationships. If we feel ugly and unlovable, we expect our partner to find our sexual impulses repulsive. When we first meet someone we find attractive, we see their best qualities. The person we love is handsome, charming, smart. If this wonderful person can love us, we believe that we must have those same qualities. At least we believe that for a little while.

After we have married the person we found so charming and lovable, we begin to see his faults. *And we may believe that he sees in us all the faults that we believe our parents saw in us.* We often react to our spouse as if he were our parents, unconsciously expecting him to treat us as our parents treated us. We cannot believe that he could find us lovable and attractive. Then we may begin to act toward him as we behaved toward our parents. Feelings of shame and resentment may appear. We may have a difficult time overcoming these feelings and allowing ourselves to enjoy our sexual desires. *Our spouse also brings feelings and expectations from his family.* He may begin to see us as being like his parents, reacting toward us as he did toward them. In the conflict that is likely to ensue, sexual pleasure is drowned out as our parents' voices fill the bedroom.

## Knowing and Communicating Our Own Desires

If we have grown up feeling that our parents are weak, vulnerable, or sad, we may feel that we needed to protect our parents, especially from our own feelings of desiring something better than they had. We develop the habit of hiding our own desires and trying to please our parents. After marriage, we may see our spouse as weak, vulnerable, or sad. We may feel that we must protect her from our desires, especially our sexual desires. We tend to see these desires as dangerous and hurtful, just as our parents experienced our desires as threatening. In a cultural climate that emphasizes the need for men to be sensitive to their wives' feelings, many men feel that they must hide their desires. The irony is that often the partner he is trying to protect has strong sexual desires that she does not feel free to express because she does not want to shock her husband with her "improper" feelings. This pattern is common in Christian couples. We find two people, each wanting a more exciting sexual life, each afraid to acknowledge these feelings to themselves or to each other.

The first step in dealing with these problems is to talk to each other. The basic approach to doing this is discussed in Chapter 17, "Other People's Feelings." We can begin to discuss our sexual feelings and fantasies with the knowledge that these fantasies are not "kinky" or "bad." Fantasies are the stories that *each and every one of us* tells himself or herself in order to create a world safe for sexual pleasure. One of the best things a couple can do is to *play a game* with their sexual fantasies, creating a scenario together in which they can act playfully toward each other in the ways that each finds exciting and each finds safe. In other words, they can share their sexual fantasies with each other and play games that create a shared world of sexual pleasure. This may seem embarrassing at first. There is a myth about "normal, healthy sexual feelings" that many of us believe that we are supposed to have. But we need to remember that *everyone's sexual fantasies and feelings feel strange to everyone else, even to one's own self.* And everyone's sexual feelings have some sort of aggressive impulse at their core, because without aggressive impulses, there would be no action.

# Boundaries

As couples begin to talk about their sexual feelings, they need to be aware of the problem of boundaries. When we first meet someone we find attractive, there is excitement in the interplay between getting to know someone and the mystery of the unknown. Each person has his or her own life. Each person has a sense of his or her own feelings and desires, and the emotional distance between the two people heightens the sexual interest. But after a couple has married, the emotional boundaries between them can begin to break down. Their lives become more intertwined and their emotions can become entangled. They begin to get inside each other's feelings. Each begins to think that he or she knows what the other is thinking and feeling, and each can begin to worry about the other person's feelings. When people begin to pay more attention to the other person's feelings than to their own, the boundaries break down. For example, they start finishing each other's sentences, often inaccurately.

What each person perceives the other's feelings to be may not be what the other person is really feeling at all. Each person begins to see his or her parents' feelings in the other person. Very often a person is attracted in the first place to someone who has the same kind of feelings that his or her parents had. For instance, girls who have been abused by their fathers are often drawn to abusive men as husbands. Men who have had depressed, sad, or resentful mothers often marry women who are depressed, sad, or resentful. Human beings have a remarkable ability to perceive another person's true nature, even when the other person is on his best behavior.

Then each person can resume the role that he or she played in his or her original family, expecting the spouse to play the part of his or her family in the hope that the Idealized Self will finally succeed in winning love from someone like its parents. Each person then operates not from his or her own feelings and desires, but from what he or she expects the other person's feelings and desires to be. *Each person is so busy trying to figure out what the other is feeling that neither is aware of his or her own feelings.* The tragedy of this situation is that the more successful the relationship, the more the couple love each other, the more likely this overidentification with each other is to occur.

Sexual excitement cannot survive unless we maintain the boundaries by paying attention to our own feelings and desires. This does not mean that we are oblivious to what the other person is feeling, taking what we want with no consideration of the other. As with all our feelings and desires, we have to be aware of our own emotions before we take into account the feelings and desires of others. We must have a real self before we can establish a genuine relationship with another person. This is especially true with our sexual feelings. Two people operating exclusively from their Idealized Selves cannot build a relationship that includes both emotional intimacy and sexual intimacy.

Some couples who become entangled in each other's feelings reestablish their boundaries by fighting. When they fight, the husband and wife push each other away by feeling that the other is wrong or bad. Once they have moved far enough apart to feel that each has his or her own feelings, they are able to make up, often by having exciting sex. If they can learn to keep their boundaries firm, they can continue to enjoy their emotional and sexual relationship without having to fight.

# Pornography

Some people are concerned about pornography. Both men and women can find themselves drawn to sexual books and Web sites, and they often feel deep shame that they cannot stop turning to them. We need to understand that what we call pornography serves to create a story in which we undo the feelings that interfere with our sexual pleasure. Women who feel unloved and unlovable often turn to romance novels in which a man is so drawn to the heroine's beauty that he is willing to do anything to possess her. This could be considered "pornography for women."

Men's stories tend to be more visual and graphic. In men's fantasies, women love sex. They are not depressed or vulnerable. Men who are afraid that their own sexual desires will harm their wives may turn to stories of women, often young girls, who delight in men's sexual feelings. Because sexual desires are so powerful, trying to stay away from these stories usually leads to being overwhelmed by stronger sexual desires and then to worse feelings of guilt. Rather than "just saying no," we need to understand what these stories mean to us.

Women are often afraid that their husbands turn to pornography because they find them unattractive. If a woman is already overwhelmed by feelings of being unlovable, she can experience devastating shame. If she can recognize that her own feelings of being unlovable are at the root of her shame, she can begin to understand and deal with her own sexual feelings rather than accuse her husband of not loving her. She can even share with her husband her own secret fantasies of being irresistible, and husband and wife can play a game in which they can enjoy each other's fantasies.

A person may be afraid that her spouse's fantasies that involve being forced to have sex or forcing others to have sex indicate a real desire for violence. Just remember that these fantasies are stories that undo the feelings that interfere with sexual pleasure. Remember that in fantasies, each person is able to control that fantasy. Nothing happens that each one does not want to have happen. If one partner does anything that the other objects to, that is not fantasy. If a husband and wife can play with the fantasies and come to feel safe with each other, they can build a powerful sexual bond with each other and find great pleasure in their sexual life. Much of what people condemn as pornography is simply sexual fantasy that does not take place in a loving or committed relationship.

## The Physical Element of Love, Desire, and Pleasure

We have talked about couples, but what about those who are single? Here we find ourselves in the midst of a raging debate. Some claim that the unmarried should repress and ignore their sexual desires or fantasies. Others claim that because we are born with sexual desires, single people should be able to satisfy those desires. Once again, this debate exists because we have lost the full understanding of how our sexuality works.

Because human beings were created to live in the material world, our emotions of love, desire, and pleasure have an ineradicable physical element. We cannot make our physical desires go away. We cannot turn our desires off at the tap. When we try to turn off our sexual desires, the result is just the opposite of what we are trying to accomplish. When we try to turn off our sexual desires, first we ignore these desires. Then something that is not overtly sexual will bring those sexual desires to our attention. In order not to feel the sexual desires, we have to push out of awareness whatever it was that brought those desires to the fore. Soon something that was not sexual by nature becomes highly sexually charged. If we find someone even mildly sexually attractive, we may find ourselves overcome with embarrassment and awkwardness because we cannot admit to ourselves that we have any sexual feelings at all. Soon we have to ignore many feelings and desires because they remind us of the sexual feelings that we are determined not to have. *Then instead of having no sexual feelings, we have nothing but sexual feelings.* In the Victorian Age, women who had been taught that they should have no sexual desires found all their emotions so sexualized that they had to faint in order to avoid any feeling that might remind them of their sexual desires.

The Victorian Age has been called an age of hypocrisy, but hypocrisy was not the problem. The problem was the idea that we can make sexual feelings go away through will power. *Using "will power" to make sexual feelings go away simply does not work.* The Idealized Self cannot stand forever against the strength of desire. Those who insist that sexual desires should exist only within marriage and only toward the spouse are those who are very likely to find themselves involved in actions they hate but feel powerless to resist.

Often when the Idealized Self cannot admit that it is besieged by such unacceptable desires, it projects these desires onto others—it is other people who have those sexual feelings. It is other people who have dirty minds and evil desires. The Idealized Self then draws itself up and refuses to understand "how anyone could do these terrible things."

In reaction to Victorian "hypocrisy" and hysteria, some have taught that sexual urges are natural and good and should be acted on without any religious guilt. The result of this is an ever larger number of people who act on their sexual desires until they lose all interest in sex. The most common sexual problem that adults complain of today is a lack of interest in sex. What people do not realize is that the attempt to deny oneself any sexual feelings except for one's spouse is the flip side of the coin of sexual hedonism. Both sides of the coin are an "all or nothing" approach to sexuality. It should be clear to everyone that neither of these approaches has had much success in integrating our sexuality into the larger context of our lives.

## The Alternative to All or Nothing

What is the alternative? Let's begin by thinking about our reactions when we see a baby. What do we feel? What do we want to do? Most often we want to reach out our arms and say, "Oh, may I hold her?" We want to cuddle the baby. We want to talk to her and smile at her. Freud caused scandal by suggesting that feelings like this were sexual. But in some sense they are. They are feelings of physical love, desire, and pleasure in the presence of a beautiful human being. Our reactions to beautiful children and beautiful adults are similar. Unless our ability to love, desire, and take pleasure in other human beings has been damaged, we feel a reaction of physical pleasure in the presence of someone we find attractive.

The culture of the United States has so sexualized our feelings of love, desire, and pleasure that we cannot believe that people can physically enjoy the presence of other people without that enjoyment somehow involving sex. Because so many Christians have tried to deny their own sexual feelings, they have become unable to experience the physical pleasure that human beings naturally feel in each other's presence because those feelings of pleasure might have a tinge of what they fear might be sexual, and therefore bad. As a result, children grow up these days starved for physical touch. When they reach adolescence, they then try to satisfy their need to be touched and held through sexual activity.

Until we are able to recognize our own physical desires— desires ranging from the pleasure of holding a baby to the pleasure of sexual desire—we will find ourselves trapped in the lies of the Idealized Self, flipping between denying that we feel any sexual desires and finding ourselves acting on those desires in ways that are embarrassing and destructive. Only when we recognize and accept our own wide range of physical desires will we be in a position to guide and direct those desires wisely in ways that serve our love of God and our neighbor.

## Sex and Teenagers

What about young people? Debates rage about sex education and sexual activity among adolescents, but these debates usually generate more heat than light. Once again, we tend to think of the problem only in terms of what is sinful and what is not sinful. This misses the point. Teenagers are engaged in the serious activity of becoming adults, and they are overwhelmed with the new feelings and desires that come with adulthood. As children they had to learn to integrate their emotions with the intellect and the will. When the desires and feelings of adulthood strike, adolescents need to reintegrate themselves, bringing adult emotions into the context of the self that they developed as children. This is a long, complicated process that is short-circuited if a teenager becomes involved in sexual behavior prematurely.

The process of integrating our feelings with the intellect and the will has one great enemy—*acting out*. A small child experiences little difference between wanting and acting. If the child never receives the love and guidance from his parents that help him to develop the space between wanting and acting, any desire becomes the occasion for taking action in order to satisfy the desire. This is called "acting out" because the emotion or desire moves outward into action before the child can understand it or guide it. If this happens, when adolescence arrives, the result can be overwhelming. Sexual urges are among the most powerful feelings we have. *Once teenagers begin acting out their sexual impulses, they stop trying to integrate them with their will and their intellect.*

The problem is especially acute when the teenager has developed an Idealized Self. The Idealized Self may try to control the desires of the pleasure emotions, but this ends in an increasingly tense standoff between the Idealized Self and the pleasure emotions. The Idealized Self may try to deny the power of the pleasure emotions until the pleasure emotions overwhelm the Idealized Self. A teenager may feel guilt and self-loathing when he can't control his impulses. Or the intensity of sexual pleasure may overwhelm him, convincing him that the values that his parents have tried to teach him are simply repressive and punitive.

We make a mistake when we simply call on teenagers to control their sexual impulses. What they need to do is to integrate their sexual impulses into the real selves that are emerging into adulthood. This allows the contemplative intellect and the loving will to make choices about sexuality that take into account both physical and spiritual goods. But when the real self is dominated by the Idealized Self, no integration can take place. If we lecture teens on morality without addressing their underlying sense of loneliness and unhappiness, without helping them to nurture their real selves, we are simply adding to their burden. The result is likely to be teens who see no relationship between the demands of morality and their own lives and experience, who reject their parents' beliefs as outdated and hypocritical. The result is also likely to be teens who end up having sexual relations when what they really want to do is cuddle up and feel close to somebody.

## Sex and the Single Person

What about unmarried adults? Many people feel that the Christian teaching that sexual activity is only for those who are married is simply wrong. After all, they say, what are single people to do with their sexual feelings and desires? Once again, we have to take into account the whole context of sexual activity rather than just focusing on the question of sin. What we have said about adolescents and sex is equally true for adults. The question is not whether or not to have sex, but rather how to integrate sexual feelings into the larger context of the real self.

In a world that stresses the pragmatic emotions and ignores the pleasure emotions, many people believe that their sexual feelings are the only feelings that are truly theirs. It seems to them that only by acting on their sexual feelings can they be who they really are. Those who demand that they deny their sexual feelings seem to take away their last shred of pleasure, their last piece of identity. Until we can hold out the promise of respect for the pleasure emotions, many will have a hard time seeing those who counsel sexual restraint as anything but mean-spirited and hardhearted.

People often experience little physical or emotional closeness outside sexual relationships. People are isolated in their cars and their cubicles. They are often far from their families. The neighborhoods and small towns of the past are long gone, and the closeness of malls and shopping is not satisfying. We need to find ways for the pleasure emotions to find physical satisfaction that is not purely sexual. We need to find true emotional depth and closeness in a social context, allowing people to find physical and emotional closeness with others, whether they are single or married, outside a sexual context. Without this, arguments about sex lead nowhere.

Many people who are not married want to be married. If someone longs to be married, it is not helpful to concentrate on what is wrong with all the men or women out there. It is better to ask, "Why am *I* not married?" There are some who are called to the single life, but more often immature emotional patterns stand in the way of marriage. How many of us get involved with the same kind of person over and over? How many of us are afraid of emotional intimacy and try to substitute physical intimacy for real emotional closeness? How many of us find ourselves in the same kind of romantic situations again and again, hoping that this time it will turn out differently? Some people find themselves involved in relationship after relationship that does not lead to marriage. Often they quickly become involved sexually. At first, the relationship seems wonderful, but it ends either with a bang or with a whimper.

If we want to be married, we need to take a look at our Idealized Self, at our real desires, at how we tried to please our parents. Marriage is a relationship between two adults. If our real self is still a frightened, suffering child, chances are that we will not be able to sustain a marriage.

Our sexual fantasies are a window into who we really are, into the emotional patterns that keep us from finding the love that we are seeking. If we listen to our sexual fantasies and let them talk to us about our real fears and desires, they can help us to know our real emotions and to integrate these emotions with our reason and will. This is the way to find the right partner.

## Listening to Your Sexuality

Human sexuality is enormously complicated. Since each person's sexual feelings and problems are unique, we could not even begin to explore the range of sexual feelings and problems in one chapter. There are some basic understandings, however, that can guide us in living with our sexual feelings and in integrating these feelings with the rest of who we are. *We can begin by reading and then rereading this book and the books we recommend in the last chapter.*

As we listen to our sexual feelings we can begin to sort them out. The first step in integrating any emotion is to recognize it. Once we recognize a desire, we can listen to it and give the desire its true voice and its true name. Human desires are never simple. Recognizing a desire sounds straightforward, but it isn't simple.

Often what we perceive as a sexual desire is really a desire for physical and emotional closeness. What we may really crave is being touched and held, especially if we didn't experience the physical closeness that babies and children need. In a culture that overvalues sexuality and scorns being needful, it is easy to turn to sexual activity to satisfy desires that are really a young child's need to be cuddled and held. *The real desire, the longing to be touched and held, is not satisfied by sexual activity.* If we impose sexual activity on these feelings, we are sexually abusing a young child, and that child is ourselves.

If a child has been deeply hurt, any feeling of love and desire can activate fear and rage. If a child has been badly abused or neglected, he will have feelings of hostility, rage, and resentment. These feelings can become deeply entangled with all desires. When these desires are the powerful desires of sex, we have a powder keg sitting right next to a lighted match. Sexuality can become the means of acting out all the hurt, all the rage that a person has felt for years. Then sex is not a way of knowing and uniting. At best, it becomes a way of relieving the hurt. People turn to sexual relationships to try to relieve the terrible feelings that grew out of the abuse and neglect. At worst, sexual acting out becomes a way of getting even by hurting others. That is why we see so many horrible examples of sexual abuse and assault.

The first step in respecting our sexual impulses is to stop when we feel them. Don't act on them. Instead, reflect. Listen to them. At first, the only thing you may hear is, "Act on me! Act on me!" But if you listen, if you follow the impulses in your fantasies where they want to go in your mind, they will tell you about themselves. One image we have found useful in doing this is the idea of putting a car in neutral. Then the engine is running, but the gears aren't engaged so the car can't take off.

You will find all kinds of memories, desires, and images coming into your mind and some of them may appall you. These are terrible, you are likely to say to yourself. How could any good person feel these things? Remember that these images and desires reflect what happened to you. If you were badly hurt as a child, you may find that you imagine hurting others. This feeling is real, but it is not all of who you are. But if you just announce to yourself that you really don't feel this way and try to banish the images, they will not go away. They will find a way to reappear because they are a real part of you, a real emotional reaction to things that really happened to you. You must recognize these emotions, feel them and listen to them, but not act them out.

## Talking about Your Sexual Feelings

As you nurture your pleasure emotions, it will become easier to sort out your sexual feelings. You will be better able to distinguish between your sexual feelings and your need to be touched and held. You also need to become aware of the role that your

Idealized Self plays in your sexual feelings. As you explore this, it is important to talk about your sexual feelings, since it is through words that we integrate our emotions with our will and our intellect. A husband and wife can share their sexual fantasies and talk to each other about their feelings. A counselor or therapist may be helpful. There are support groups for those who have been abused. You may be able to talk to a friend. Writing out your feelings can be helpful. If you have no one else to talk to about these feelings, talk to God. Tell him what you are feeling. He already knows, but in telling him, you are actively sharing the feelings in a conversation with another person. Remember that as you deal with all of your feelings, you will be able to understand and deal with your sexual feelings more easily.

## Sex and Children

What about our children? How can we help them to deal with their sexuality? We have to begin when they are young. We need to give them the physical affection they need, to accept their feelings, and to help them to guide their own emotions and to know what they really want. We will talk about how to do this in the next chapter.

We need to talk to our children about sex. This does not mean dumping adult information on small children. Children are usually aware of what they want to know and need to know. Remember the old joke about the five-year-old who asked where he came from. After his father told him all about sex, the kid replied, "Gee, Tommy said he came from Detroit." It is always a good idea, if a child asks a broad question, to ask him exactly what he wants to know. On the other hand, our media present sexual images and information (and misinformation) to children at an early age. We can no longer wait to give our children "the talk" when they reach adolescence. Children need accurate information about sex long before they become teenagers.

Children are exposed to images and experiences that are overwhelming, far beyond what they can deal with at their stage of emotional development. It is important to protect children from these images as much as possible, not because they are bad (although some of them are), but because they are inappropriate to the child's age. We do not expect a child to pilot a jet plane. Why do we expect children to deal with adult sexual feelings when their own feelings are not yet mature? Since it is almost impossible to protect children totally, it is important to talk to them. If they have seen or experienced something that has disturbed them or that is beyond their comprehension, listen and accept what they have to say. Don't get angry or excited yourself, lest you compound their feelings of being disturbed. Let them know how much you love them and give them an explanation suitable to their development.

The most important thing you can do to help your children to deal with their sexuality is to face your own feelings about sex. Children are enormously sensitive to their parents' feelings, often knowing them better than the parents themselves do. If your sexual feelings are tied in with feelings of hostility, your children will pick this up. If you are fearful of sex, your children will know this. These feelings will play into their growing sexuality, working themselves out in ways you do not expect. Acting out your own sexual feelings is the one sure way to encourage sexual acting out in your children.

# 22
# Our Children, Our Selves

Our children are in some sense an extension of our selves. They come from within us. They carry us within their genetic makeup. We give them life. We are responsible for bringing them up. They bring us happiness and they bring us sorrow. One of the things that people most often wish they could change is the way they treat their children.

Modern research in child development points out that the most important thing that a mother can do is to fall deeply in love with her child, to be absolutely certain that this is the most wonderful, most perfect, most adorable baby in the whole world. Responding to this love, the baby loves his mother in turn.

Many things can happen to interfere with this love. A child may be born imperfect or with an inborn way of sensing the world that differs radically from his mother's. But the most common problem a mother has in expressing her love for her child comes when she carries within herself the unresolved emotional hurts of her own upbringing. A mother who did not receive the love that she needed from her own mother finds it difficult, if not impossible, to love her baby with that spontaneous, all-encompassing love that a child needs.

Often without realizing it, parents expect their children to give them the love that they never received from their own parents. Children do love their parents, but the kind of love that a child has for his parents is not the same love that parents have for their children. Children, themselves needing love and nurture, simply are not capable of giving nurturing love. It is very, very difficult for a mother who was not loved and nurtured to give a child the love and nurture that he needs. The mother's own needs and her Idealized Self interfere with her relationship with her child whether she wants them to or not. No matter how many times she has promised herself that she will never, never be like her own mother, she is often horrified to hear her mother's words popping out of her mouth before she can stop them.

Sometimes a mother experiences her child's needs as overwhelming. Her baby can seem clinging and demanding. It is true that some children need more attention than others, but *if a mother experiences a young baby as clinging and demanding, chances are that she is struggling with her own need to be mothered.* If she is able to recognize this, she has already helped her child. When she experiences her baby as causing her distress, the baby senses this and feels that she is disappointed in him, that he is not a lovable baby. If a mother can recognize that she did not receive the love that she needed, she can use her intellect to figure out how to deal with the situation. She can listen to her own emotions, feel her own sense of loss, and mourn her own suffering and deprivation. She can accept her own feelings and stop blaming herself because she does not feel the kind of love for her child that she had hoped to feel. She can figure out how to find gratification for her own needs, whether getting a massage or having someone care for her, at least some of the time, as she cares for her baby. She can turn to her husband for understanding and support. What she is able to do depends on her situation, but the important thing is to recognize that the problem lies in her own feelings, not in her baby, and that *her feelings are neither her fault nor her baby's fault.* Her baby, as young as he is, will know this. Recent research demonstrates the amazing grasp babies have of feelings. She can even talk to him, telling him that she is feeling bad because her mother couldn't love her, but that he is a wonderful baby and she loves him very much. As young as the child is, he will understand this.

When a mother feels overwhelmed by her inability to meet her child's needs, she can identify with her child and then enjoy, as if she were the child, the love that she is giving him. She can picture herself as her baby and allow herself to experience this care as if she *were* the baby. This process helps her to meet the child's needs and to grow in love as she receives some of the love she gives the child. Psychoanalysts call this process sublimation. It works.

# Working on Our Emotional Development

*The first thing we need to do for our children is to work on our own emotional development. If we do not take responsibility for our own emotional development, we will dump our emotional problems on our children whether we mean to or not.* We cannot be perfect parents, but children know when their parents are refusing to face their own emotional problems and are acting them out instead. Children also know when their parents are struggling not to act out, even when the struggle is not successful. When we fall short, we can tell our children that we have not done all that needed to be done. If we see that we have been unfair or hurtful, we can acknowledge it and apologize. In this way, we can show our children that we are struggling to grow, and we can show them that they, too, can fall short, say they are sorry, and go on to do better. This can minimize the need to feel guilty.

*As we work on our own emotional development, we need to nurture our own humane emotions.* If we are aware of what we desire and we do our best to understand and integrate our desires, we are less likely to project our desires onto our children. If we are entangled in our own Idealized Self, we often try to create an ideal child who will satisfy our own neurotic needs instead of loving our child just for who he is.

When we want something for our children, we need to ask ourselves whether we want this for our children or for ourselves. If, for instance, we want our children to love classical music, we need to ask ourselves why. Is it because we wish that we had studied music when we were little? Because we feel deprived, are we determined that our children won't be deprived? We need to remember that *whatever we give to our children, we also give them the emotion with which we give it.* If we give our children something out of the sense of our own deprivation, the feeling of deprivation will cling to whatever we give them. If we give our children something out of resentment that we didn't get but wanted when we were little, the feeling of resentment will contaminate the gift.

*If we feel deprived of something—music lessons, French classes, a chance to play basketball—we should give it to ourselves.* In that way, we nurture our own humane emotions. If we do something because we love it, there is a much better chance that our children will love it, too. Young children love what those around them love. When children love their parents, they want to be like them. They mimic and copy them, putting on their clothes, begging to be allowed to plant the flowers, or dribble the ball, or play the piano.

## Helping a Child to Know What He Wants

*Parents need to help children to know their own desires.* Children seem to like the strangest things. Parents can have a hard time knowing what particular aspect of a child's desire is the key to his interest. For instance, if a child shows an interest in beetles, his parents might run out and get books on entomology and cases for collecting insects, taking over the child's interest and overwhelming it. It may not be insects that fascinate the child, but the glorious colors of beetles.

*If a child follows his own interests and desires, no matter how odd or unproductive they may appear to his parents, he will follow those interests and desires to the life that God has imagined for him.* In following their own interests and skills, children develop their humane emotions. Many parents have been amazed to see that some interest or inclination that they thought was frivolous or silly has turned out to be the child's way to happiness and real success.

In a world where resumé building begins in kindergarten, parents often push their children into sports, activities, and lessons out of a fear that the child will fall behind and not be able to make it in a dog-eat-dog competitive world. If we do this, we encourage the premature development of the pragmatic emotions, which encourages the child's Idealized Self. If a child feels loved and if his pleasure emotions are allowed to develop, the pragmatic emotions will follow, taking their proper place in the child's development.

# Accepting a Child's Feelings

A child needs to feel loved just for who he is. *An essential part of this is accepting the child's feelings.* A young child's feelings are who he is. He loves, he hates, he wants, he rejects. These are his pleasure emotions and these emotions are the core of who we are. *When a parent is afraid of a child's feelings or responds to a child's feelings with rejection and disapproval, the child feels that he is being rejected.* A young child is not able to draw the adult distinction between who he is and what he feels. He *is* his feelings. If his parents reject his feelings, he will try desperately to change those feelings to please his parents. This is the beginning of the Idealized Self.

Many parents believe that accepting a child's feelings is the same as allowing the child to act out those feelings. They believe that the way to change a child's behavior is to change the feelings behind the behavior. They often sincerely believe that to insist that a child do something that he does not want to do is coercive and manipulative. Often these parents had parents who valued obedience and disregarded their children's feelings. Trying to avoid their own parents' mistake, they try to get their young child to understand their point of view and to want what they want him to want. Unfortunately, young children really want what they themselves want. They want what seems good to them. *If we try to make a child feel what we want him to feel, we are telling the child that the feelings that he really does have—his own desires and emotions—are bad.*

Because young children long so desperately for their parents' love and approval, a child will deny his own feelings, his own desires, even his own perceptions to try to win his parents' approval and love. But approval given on the condition that a child change what he feels is approval that teaches the child to lie to himself and to others. If a child experiences his parents as rejecting his desires and emotions, he will not feel loved, no matter what his parents' motives are in disapproving of these desires and emotions.

Some parents, afraid of their own feelings of hostility, react negatively to any evidence of anger in their children. They may react to anger with rage or condemnation, or they may withdraw emotionally from the child. This does not create a child who feels no anger. This results in a child full of hostility and fear. If we try to get rid of a child's emotions or try to turn them into emotions we approve of, we do great damage.

Jim has heard many stories from people who have abandoned their parents' faith. Over and over again, people have said, "I was sick of having religion rammed down my throat." Some parents conclude from this that it is better not to teach a child any particular religion. Better, they say, to let the child decide for himself when he gets older. This is like waiting until he gets older to teach him mathematics if he resists learning arithmetic when he is young. The problem is not religion. The problem is that religious parents, often with the best of intentions, deny their children's emotions in the name of religion. When the children grow up and want to reclaim their own emotions, they think it is necessary to reject religion in order to be who they are. They assume that denying who they are is at the heart of religion, since it was in the name of religion that their parents rejected their emotions. The problem is often compounded by parents' hostility. A parent who is full of hostility, and who fails to deal with his own emotions, is likely to use whatever he values most—religion, academics, music, sports—as an instrument of hostility toward his children. This hostility calls forth hostile resistance in the children.

## Guiding a Child's Emotions and Actions

But, parents respond, you can't just let a child do whatever he wants. This is true. Children do need guidance. Small children have intellects, but the intellects do not see very far. The reasoning process needs time to develop. The brain and nervous system are not complete at birth, and they continue developing for some years. In fact, human beings are not completely mature physically until some time in their twenties. *Parents need to act as the child's intellect, guiding his emotions and his actions.*

The child must not be allowed to do whatever he wants because he often can't know the consequences of what he wants. No matter how much he wants to pick up the cat by the tail, it is not a good idea. One way to think about guiding children is to ask ourselves if the behavior we think is cute when they are small will be cute when they are sixteen. Taking into account the child's stage of development, we need to guide him in developing the habits that will best serve him when he is older. If we allow children to behave in a hostile manner, hurting animals for instance, we are allowing them to develop the habit of cruelty. If we encourage them to eat junk food whenever they want to, we are encouraging them to develop habits that will be detrimental to their health throughout their entire lives.

Too many parents are afraid to guide and discipline their children because they are afraid that their children will be mad at them, that their children won't love them. They are partly right. A very young child reacts with anger if he is stopped from doing what he wants to do. Before the age of around two, it is as if there were two mothers. There is the "good" mother who is always smiling, and the child loves that mother with a pure, unadulterated love. There is also, in the child's mind, the "bad" mother who thwarts him, and he can resent that mother with all his heart. It is as if he is incapable of understanding that these two are the very same mother. The mother who gives him good things is good, while the mother who thwarts him is bad. If the child receives the guidance he needs, he eventually realizes that the good mother and the bad mother are the same mother, and he learns the amazing fact that the same person can seem good and bad at different times. This is one of the foundations of abstract reasoning. This is also the beginning of the perception of ambivalence, the realization that one can feel two different ways about the same person or thing.

Many parents cannot bear the force of a child's anger when he feels thwarted. Because their own emotions were not accepted, it doesn't occur to them to simply accept the child's feelings. Because they did not receive sufficient love and acceptance, they expect the child to somehow provide that love. When he is full of anger at being thwarted, they don't understand that after the anger subsides, his love for his parents will break through again. They are terrified of losing what love he can give them. So they cave in, giving him whatever he wants. Later on, they are amazed that he does not seem to love them, but continues to rage and demand things. Caving in to his anger teaches him that a tantrum gets results. This is one example of the harm that parents can do when they are unaware of their own needs and fears. If parents do not accept and guide the child's anger, neither condemning it nor giving in to it, the child will never learn to guide his own anger or to accept that he cannot have whatever he desires whenever he desires it.

Some parents react to a child's anger with their own rage, trying to beat down his anger with violence or punishment. The result of this is a child filled with hostility, resentment, bitterness, and rage. The rage may be covered over by a thick layer of fear, since children are terrified of their parents' rage or rejection. But when parents react to their children's anger with condemnation or rage, the result is not children who are full of love.

## Breaking a Child's Will

It is important to talk about an idea that once played a major part in child-raising—the idea of breaking a child's will. According to this idea, a child must be taught obedience, and willfulness stands in the way of obedience. The will was equated with resistance. By breaking a child's will, parents hoped to create a docile, pliant, good child. Some parents, in response to their own parents' attempt to break their will, decided that it was better not to discipline children at all. It is important to look at what breaking a child's will implies and what the results are.

This idea rested on a mistaken understanding of the will. It assumed that the desires of childhood, primarily desires for the good things that the senses perceive, were necessarily in conflict with the desire for the higher things of the spirit. This assumption rested in turn on the idea that the flesh and the spirit must be at war with each other. Parents believed that the will should be a tyrant, crushing out the desires of the pleasure emotions in order to allow the spirit to gain strength. But God created our loving will and our pleasure emotions to love him with the same intensity with which we love our parents, the sweetness of honey, or the warm sun after a long winter. If we suppress the loving will and the pleasure emotions, we cripple our love for God and for other human beings.

The will is a desire for what is spiritually good. This desire develops out of a child's love for his parents and for the good things that God has created. *If a child's will is broken, his ability to love is broken.* He may obey out of fear or habit, but he will not love God or his neighbor. If the pleasure emotions are crushed, they do not go away. They are overwhelmed by feelings of rage, resentment, hostility, and bitterness that are cut off from the guidance of the intellect and the will. The rage, hostility, resentment, and bitterness are often projected outward. A person whose pleasure emotions have been damaged by an attempt to break his will often cannot bear to recognize his own hostility. He must see the emotions he fears in himself in someone else. If you listen to him, he sounds paranoid.

*Often a parent projects the emotions that he senses and fears in himself onto one of his children, most often the oldest child.* He then decides that the child must be disciplined in order to drive out the evil. In this way, the parent creates in his child the very emotions of hostility, resentment, rage, and bitterness that he fears in himself. The cycle of hostility goes on and on, each generation visiting its rage on the next, even to the seventh generation.

# Dialogue with a Baby

How do we go about guiding children? *First we must listen to the child and try to understand and accept his emotions.* How do we listen to a child who can't talk? Children communicate through their emotions. We can tune in to the feelings of the tiniest baby. When a baby cries, it is his way of communicating. He is saying that he is uncomfortable or that he wants something. Many parents are driven frantic by their child's crying. They fear that something is wrong, and they feel inadequate when they can't stop him from crying. They check his diaper, offer food, check to see if he has a fever or if something is causing discomfort. The child keeps crying, often until he is picked up and carried.

This is often what the child is trying to communicate—that he is lonely. After all, he spent nine months going everywhere with his mother. Suddenly he is ejected into a cold, strange place where he has to learn how to eat, how to sleep, how to breathe, and how to regulate his own body temperature. He is overwhelmed and uncomfortable. He is separated from his mother. When she goes away, he has no way of knowing how long she will be away or even that she will come back. If his mother is distressed, he can feel this and cannot possibly understand why she is distressed. He just knows that it feels terrible to him.

But we can talk to the child. The child does not understand words, but he understands feelings. When we talk to the child, our words and demeanor carry our feelings. We can tell him that we love him, that we want to know what is distressing him, and that we want to take care of him. We can carry him and sing to him. We can reassure him when we put him down that we will be back. We can take his crying seriously as the child's way of speaking to us instead of seeing the crying as a condemnation of our ability as parents.

If a mother is able to feel her love for her child, she reaches out to him, encouraging him to respond to her. This begins a dialogue between mother and child. *This dialogue between mother and child is the most important thing in the world to the child.* Young children want to be with their mothers all the time. They cry when their mothers go away. This is not clinging and whining. When a mother turns her child over to someone else, the child often cries until the mother is out of sight. This is the child's effort to persuade his mother not to leave. It is in the dialogue between mother and child that the child learns to be a human being, a member of the human race. If this dialogue does not take place, the child's heart is left empty and cold, and there is nothing on earth that can fill it.

## Dialogue with a Child

This dialogue takes place first through the physical care that the mother gives the child and through the emotions that they share in the course of that care. The situation becomes more complex when the child reaches the "terrible twos" and begins to discover his ability to "just say no." It is at this point that a mother's ability to accept her child's feelings, while at the same time guiding his behavior, becomes critical. A mother can make clear to her child that he doesn't have to *want* to do something such as brushing his teeth, but he does have to do it. If a child knows that he is loved, he will be better able to accept the guidance, because a *parent's authority rests on love.*

If a child feels loved, it is easier for him to believe that what his parents require of him is for his own benefit. He is able to accept his parents' guidance because he loves them and wants to be like them. If a child does not feel loved and accepted for who he is, he experiences his parents' requirements as arbitrary demands that he must obey to earn their love. This is not to say that if a child feels loved, he will not resist what his parents expect of him. A two-year-old is beginning the process of defining who he is, of establishing his own boundaries, and the word *no* is an important part of that process. If a child feels that his parents accept his emotions, he is better able to handle the process of negotiating with his parents, of working out with them the boundary where his own desires run up against what he has to do to live with others in love.

If a child does not feel that his parents accept his feelings, the child can only alternate between denying his own feelings in order to win his parents' love and stubbornly asserting his own feelings in an attempt to establish the right for those feelings to exist. This leads to a struggle between parent and child for the power to define the child's emotions. The resulting Idealized Self may be sweet and obedient or it may be aggressive and contrary, but underlying that Idealized Self will be a pool of hostility, resentment, rage, and bitterness.

## Finding Out What Children Are Really Saying

Parents are often afraid of their children's feelings. A child may say something like, "I hate you," or "I'm bad." Parents often rush to correct the child's feelings, saying something like, "It isn't nice to hate people," or "No, you're good." Instead, a parent can say something like, "I wonder why you feel as if you hate me right now," or "I wonder why you think you're bad right now." *What the child is actually feeling can be quite different from what the parent assumes that the child is feeling.*

When a parent really listens to what the child is feeling, the parent can continue the dialogue with the child. If a child says, "I hate you. I don't want to clean up my room," the parent can respond with, "It's okay if you resent having to clean up your room. It isn't as much fun to clean up your room as it is to go out and play. But cleaning up your room is your share of taking care of the place where we all live together, and you need to do it. If you hurry, you might still have time to go out and play." Or she might say, "Would you like me to help you?"

If the child says, "I'm bad. I just hit my sister," the parent can respond by saying, "It's good that you see that hitting your sister is a problem. Maybe you can tell me why you felt like hitting her." Jim has observed more than one mother respond to her son by telling him that he was really good after he had told her that he was bad. Then a few seconds later, the boy's sister reported that he had hit her. The boy was trying to tell his mother about his bad behavior, but she contradicted his feelings before he could express all of them.

It is through this constant daily dialogue that a child comes to recognize his own emotions and to develop the ability to guide those emotions by himself. It is a long and difficult process, but it is enormously rewarding.

## The Importance of Good Habits

*Within this process of having a dialogue with a child, parents need to help him to develop good habits.* The patterns of behavior that a child develops when he is young stay with him throughout his life. If a child learns that he can make people do what he wants by nagging, he will probably continue to do this into adolescence and possibly into adulthood. If he develops the habit of drinking soda and eating cookies to the exclusion of nutritious food, he will keep right on eating them. If he can avoid doing anything his parents ask him to do, he will avoid doing what his teachers and employers ask him to do. If a child learns early to enjoy vegetables and fruits and to avoid sweets, he will not have to struggle against his cravings later in life. If he learns to pick up after himself, he will not have to live in a chaotic house as an adult. If he learns to be kind and thoughtful of others, he will avoid a great deal of conflict with others throughout his life.

Parents should encourage a child in his impulse to be active in order to develop the habit of being active. They should support him in playing the sports that appeal to him, whether or not they are the sports that appeal to his parents.

## The Importance of Beauty

*We want to emphasize the enormous importance of surrounding children with what is beautiful and good.* What a child sees and hears forms his imagination. The imagination is the repository of all that we experience and the foundation of our humane emotions and our intellect. In the contemporary world, children's imaginations are formed by images of violence and sex. A child prepares himself to live in the world by observing the world, and he absorbs what he observes without thinking about it. If a child observes only ugliness, violence, rage, and sexual acting out, he incorporates these things into himself. He then finds it difficult to believe that beauty, love, and goodness are real. Why should he believe in goodness when his own experience and observation tell him that the world is full of hostility and violence? The Greek philosopher Plato taught that the most effective education for a child is playing among lovely things.

It is critical, therefore, that children experience beauty. This does not have to be classical music or copies of Rembrandt's paintings, although these are wonderful. Gospel music, mariachi music, African drumming. Children's books, photographs, cleverly painted furniture. A. A. Milne's *Now We Are Six,* "The Midnight Ride of Paul

Revere," nursery rhymes. A few flowers in a vase, a responsive pet, walks in the park, an enjoyable and playful game. All of these nurture the pleasure emotions and support the development of the humane emotions.

Raising children is the hardest work we do. It is also one of the greatest pleasures that God has given us—the chance to do what he does, to love and nurture those most amazing of all creatures, human beings.

# 23
# Jim's List

This book presents a lot of material. It can be hard to remember all that we have said, and you will need to read the book over and over in order to get the full good out of it. In the meantime, there are things that you can do to feel better right now. If you are feeling depressed, resentful, agitated, anxious, or stressed:

1. Remember Henry David Thoreau's maxim: "Simplify, simplify, simplify." Simplify your life.
2. Moderate your use of alcohol, coffee, tea, and foods that contain sugar and refined carbohydrates. Avoid so-called recreational drugs.
3. Get plenty of exercise by walking, running, swimming, or bicycling—up to an hour and a half a day if you are depressed. Even a half hour of exercise helps.
4. Reduce stress, especially the kind that involves deadlines. Catch up on your obligations.
5. Restore order to your life. Wash your car, polish your shoes, pay your bills, tidy up your home.
6. Spend time by yourself getting in touch with your feelings.
7. Don't *try* to do it. *Do* it.

# 24
# Books That Help

If we tried to include all the ideas that we have found helpful, this book would be very, very long. Many people have said what needs to be said far better than we could say it. So we are suggesting a reading list.

The first books we suggest that you read are *Our Inner Conflicts* and *Neurosis and Human Growth* by Karen Horney, MD. These books deal with our defenses, the tactics that human beings use to cope with the hurts they suffer when they are young. Karen Horney describes the Idealized Self, the various patterns of behavior with which we try to earn love, patterns that are very destructive to us and to those around us. It is important to be as aware as possible of these patterns of behavior so that we can stop acting them out—acting on the feelings without being aware of what they really mean—and get behind these defenses to the real emotions we are defending ourselves against having to feel. Many people find *Our Inner Conflicts* easier to read. If you find yourself having trouble with the first chapter, skip it and come back to it later. *It is very helpful to read at least one of these books.*

Because so much of the suffering we experience originates in our earliest years, the books by Stanley I. Greenspan, MD, are very helpful. *The Irreducible Needs of Children: What Every Child Must Have to Grow, Learn, and Flourish* was written with T. Barry Brazelton, MD. Another book by Dr. Greenspan is *First Feelings: Milestones in the Emotional Development of Your Baby and Child*. These books describe what children need in each level of their development. This is helpful in enabling us to understand our children's development and to act in such a way that our children can really experience the love we have for them. These books are also helpful in understanding exactly what is lacking in our own development. If we can better pinpoint what we experienced as children, we are better able to hear what our emotions are telling us about what they need in order to grow beyond the point at which the Idealized Self began to take over. Finally, Dr. Greenspan's *The Growth of the Mind and the Endangered Origins of Intelligence* gives an overview of the latest research in child development and of how our modern culture is putting our children at risk.

Another book is *Please Understand Me* by David Keirsey and Marilyn Bates. This book describes the various temperament types. Temperament is the particular way of responding to the world that each of us was born with. This is different from personality, which is the way of responding to the world that we have developed through our experiences. Some of us, extroverts, are born preferring to be with lots of people. Some, introverts, are born preferring to be alone with our thoughts or with just one other person. Some people make decisions on the basis of their feelings, some on the basis of their thoughts. Since there are sixteen basic temperament types, differences in temperament within a family are common. One cause of conflict between parents and children is the parents' lack of understanding of how their children experience the world if their children's way is very different from their own. This book explains these different ways in which people see the world. It can also be very helpful in our own development since many of us have been harsh with ourselves because we don't react to our surroundings in the same way that other people do. Most people find it exciting to have a clear understanding of what their own temperament actually is. Two other books by David Keirsey are also available: *Please Understand Me II: Temperament, Character, Intelligence* and *Portraits of Temperament.*

Another helpful book is *What Color Is Your Parachute?* by Richard Bolles, a former pastor who found his vocation in writing this book. This book is intended to help people to discover the kind of work they most enjoy doing and to find employment doing that kind of work. Many have found it helpful in just finding out who they are. The exercises in the first part of the book explore what it was that we enjoyed doing as we grew up. Since the center of our emotional and spiritual life is the trio of love, desire, and joy, remembering what we have loved, what we have desired, and what we have enjoyed can help us to escape from the tyranny of always thinking about what we should want and should do. As you do the exercises, listen to your emotions and think about what they are telling you. Don't rush out and get caught up in more action. The purpose of doing the exercises is not just to find a job, but to discover what you love to do. Concentrate on what has brought you pleasure and how you can bring that pleasure into your life again and incorporate it into your vocation.

*Boundaries: When to Say YES, When to Say NO to Take Control of Your Life* by Dr. Henry Cloud and Dr. John Townsend is an excellent book. Maggie Scarf's book *Intimate Worlds: Life inside the Family* does a wonderful job of explaining family dynamics. *The Nature of Music: Beauty, Sound, and Healing* by Maureen McCarthy Draper gives suggestions for using music for emotional healing. A very helpful book in dealing with sexual feelings is *Arousal: The Secret Logic of Sexual Fantasies* by Dr. Michael J. Bader. *A Pattern Language* by Christopher Alexander explores the patterned relationship between people's homes and their lives.

We have found *Psychic Wholeness and Healing: Using ALL the Powers of the Human Psyche* by Anna A. Terruwe, MD, and Conrad W. Baars, MD, helpful in understanding the pleasure emotions and the pragmatic emotions. Finally, *Virtuous Passions: The*

*Formation of Christian Character* by G. Simon Harak gives a philosophical and theological foundation for our work.

While these books are all very helpful, they are not the only helpful books. God knows all books, and he will often lead you to the book that will be most helpful in your healing at any particular point. Remember that we are all different. Read, study, pray.

God longs to help us more than we could ever long to be helped. We have been promised, "Ask, and it will be given you; search, and you will find; knock, and the door will be opened for you" (Matt 7:7). Ask, search, knock. God is waiting to answer.